PRAISE FOR *TH*

"*The Pacific Northwest Reader* is a wonderful collection by a group of writers whose keen eye for place and story bursts from these sharp essays. From bookish nostalgias set in cold and soggy places to the poignant story of a clown looking for a connection, this is a great read."

—Jess Walter, author of *The Financial Lives of the Poets* and *Citizen Vince*

"I know the creators of these true stories. They work in the bookstores I visit every day. I chat with them, we tell jokes and talk about the business, and debate which book is happening and which book is hot and what's coming next. I suspected some of them were writers, but I had no idea they were so darned good! These personal tales are fantastic, fun, and delightful on their own; they're a wonderful patchwork quilt of the region when taken as a whole. I loved this collection!"

—Garth Stein, author of *The Art of Racing in the Rain* and *Raven Stole the Moon*

A portion of the proceeds from the sale of *The Pacific Northwest Reader* will go to ABFFE, the American Booksellers Foundation for Free Expression.

• • •

For a searchable directory of independent bookstores nearest you, as well as a list of the highly influential and selective Indie Next Great Reads, please visit www.IndieBound.org.

• • •

For daily news about goings-on in the publishing and bookselling world, you can subscribe to a free daily email at www.Shelf-Awareness.com and the free weekly Bookselling This Week at www.bookweb.org.

THE PACIFIC NORTHWEST READER

brought to you by

The Pacific Northwest Independent Booksellers Association

Edited by Carl Lennertz

DELPHINIUM BOOKS

HARRISON, NEW YORK • ENCINO, CALIFORNIA

THE PACIFIC NORTHWEST READER

Printed in the United States of America.

First Edition

Designed by Greg Mortimer

ISBN: 978-1-883285-41-8

CONTENTS

Editor's Note vii
Acknowledgments x

ALASKA

Alaska Steam • Melanie Colletti 5

A Walk with Dinah • Annie Tupek 17

The Hunt • John M. Libal 27

IDAHO

Blue Eden • Marcia Vanderford 41

The Spirit of Idaho • Judith Lohrey Wutzke 49

OREGON

Finding Bayocean • Gigi Little 57

3,000 Miles WNW • Colin Rea 73

Honeychild • April Nabholz 81

The Colors of Oregon • Kimberly Seits 95

Land of Oz • Karen Munro 101

Oregon Haikus • Shirley Thomas 111

WASHINGTON

Washington Ghost Story • Rem Ryals 115

Bigfoot Calls • Matthew Simmons 127

Dreaming of Rain • Sarah Hutton 135

The Rock • Ann Combs 145

My Washington ID • David K. Wheeler 151

The Wilmot Memorial Library • Susan Scott 161

A letter from Chris Finan of ABFFE 165

Directory of Pacific Northwest independent bookstores 166

Delphinium reading group suggestions 189

EDITOR'S NOTE

Seventy-five years ago, Franklin Delano Roosevelt put a who's who of writers to work chronicling every nook and cranny of America in the famous Works Progress Administration's State and City guides. In 2008, Matt Weiland and Sean Wilsey revived the idea in a book they commissioned entitled *State by State: A Panoramic Portrait of America*, published by Ecco. It features original essays by a new generation of writers, including Dave Eggers on Illinois, Ann Patchett on Tennessee, William T. Vollmann on California, and many more. This modern take on the Federal Writers' Project was not meant to be exhaustive but rather highly personal, almost impressionistic; an attempt to reveal something of the essence of each state today.

Inspired by *State by State*'s example, and in tribute to the extraordinary local knowledge of booksellers and librarians, we have now commissioned a volume on each of the rich and varied regions of America—

written by independent booksellers and librarians. These are professionals who deal with other writers' words every day of their working lives, but who don't often get a chance to see their own words in a bound book—for sale in a bookstore or to be borrowed from a library shelf. Some have had their work published in magazines or journals; for others, this is their debut.

The Great Lakes Reader came out in late 2009, and now you hold *The Pacific Northwest Reader* in your hands. Herein you will find personal and passionate essays about living in Alaska, Idaho, Oregon, and Washington—slices of life from an area bound by weather, an independent streak, and strains of American history as wild as its geography.

There is no attempt here to summarize an entire state in an essay or three, nor would that be possible. These are idiosyncratic episodes, either from those with deep roots in the Pacific Northwest or from newcomers to the region. Another intriguing feature of this book is the range in age of the contributors, as well as experiences that are perhaps foreign to you, from hitchhiking with a mule to going hunting in Alaska. (Spoiler alert: no animals get shot.) There is much in these pages about life and death, regret and happiness, nostalgia and fresh starts.

As I had to say in the introduction to *The Great Lakes Reader*, there is some geographical hairsplitting here.

Some would consider Idaho as much a part of the Rocky Mountains as the Pacific Northwest, but its bookstores belong to the Pacific Northwest Booksellers Association and some online sources classify Idaho as being part of the Northwest. Montana also belongs to the Pacific Northwest in terms of bookstore membership, but we're going to put it squarely into a forthcoming *Rocky Mountains Reader*. (Perhaps we should just dodge the issue and call this *The Lewis & Clark Reader*?) Either way, I believe you'll find that same adventurous spirit in these true tales from the area's book people.

Look for more regional volumes written by booksellers and librarians from around the country this year and next; this is the second of nine books in the series. Enjoy!

Carl Lennertz

ACKNOWLEDGMENTS

We'd like to thank the following groups and people:

The Pacific Northwest Booksellers Association, whose store member lists are in the back of this book. Thom Chambliss, the executive director, helped us tremendously in all ways, and Brian Juenemann, also of the association, gathered the state facts that grace each section.

Partners Book Distributors, for getting this book into bookstores quickly and efficiently.

The American Booksellers Association for their advocacy and marketing programs on behalf of independent bookstores all across the United States.

The librarians of America, who bring the joy of reading to every small town and big city in this country.

Greg Mortimer of Ecco, who donated his time to design the book cover and interior layout.

Mary Beth Constant of HarperCollins, who donated her time to copyedit the text.

Delphinium Books, an independent literary press, for funding the printing of this book. (See the back for listings and descriptions of their recent books.)

And finally, to the contributors to this book, who donated their time and words so this volume could be published in support of free speech, the rich legacies of their home states, and their fellow booksellers and librarians.

THE PACIFIC NORTHWEST READER

ALASKA

STATE NICKNAME The Last Frontier or Land of the Midnight Sun

STATE MOTTO "North to the Future"

STATE SONG "Alaska's Flag"

STATE ANIMAL Moose

STATE FISH King salmon

STATE FOSSIL Woolly mammoth

STATE TREE Sitka spruce

STATE SPORT Dog mushing

STATE TRIVIA:

• Mt. McKinley, at 20,320 feet, is the highest point in the U.S.

• Purchased from the Russian Empire in 1867, Alaska was not declared a state until 1959.

• Alaska has a longer coastline than all the other U.S. states combined.

• Alaska is larger than the combined area of the next three largest states: Texas, California and Montana. It is also larger than the combined area of the 22 smallest

U.S. states.

• Juneau, the state capital, has no road access to the rest of the state. It can only be reached by air or sea.

• The Trans-Alaska oil pipeline is 800 miles long, 48 inches in diameter, and crosses 834 rivers and streams, three major mountain ranges and an earthquake fault line.

• Alaska's name is derived from the Aleut word *alaxsxaq*, meaning "the object towards which the action of the sea is directed." It is also known as *Alyeska*, the "great land," another Aleut word derived from the same root.

• The numbers show that Alaskans eat more ice cream on the average than residents of any other state. (This according to Seth Kantner.)

• Famous Alaskans: Sydney Laurence, Marty Beckerman, Jewel, Carlos Boozer, Irene Bedard, Elizabeth Peratrovich, Margaret Murie, Tom Bodett, Susan Butcher, Tommy Moe

Alaska Steam

MELANIE COLLETTI

I became a part of Skagway, Alaska, during the summers I worked there. Like the broad green elephant-ear leaves of devil's club that flourish in the temperate rainforests of southeast Alaska, I sprung up quickly, thrived in the subtle drizzle and long days of summer, then curled down, retreating to the safety of the rich black dirt of winter, not to be seen again until the following spring. During winters back in Colorado, I read Robert Service and Jack London because they seemed to understand the sickness and the sadness that welled up spontaneously when thinking about Alaska.

There's a land – oh it beckons and beckons,

And I want to go back – and I will.

—From "The Spell of the Yukon" by Robert Service

With a year-round population of less than a thousand, the town of Skagway brimmed over with nearly an equal number of seasonal employees in the summers, hired to take cruise ship passengers on hiking excursions, raft trips, brothel tours, and train rides. I can close my eyes and still smell the diesel smoke of the trains and hear the deep booms of a cruise ship pulling away from town. And then comes the longing, the lingering, and vivid memories that I return to again and again, even now, years later.

I was a tour guide on the White Pass & Yukon Route railroad for two of my four summers in Skagway. Most days, three trains would haul cruise ship passengers from the docks to the summit of White Pass and back, a three-and-a-half hour round-trip. In the mornings the engineers, conductors, and brakemen would put together the trains, restored vintage parlor cars pulled by yellow and green 1950s diesel engines. They backed the trains down to the depot where the tour guides—me and the other twenty- or thirty-somethings not yet resigned to year-round work or graduate degrees—would hop on to prepare the trains for the day. A few of us would lug bags of soda and bottled water up the hanging metal steps, while others flipped the bench seats over to face forward for the trip up the pass, putting a tour booklet on each of the seats. We also had to test the microphone, which would later carry a guide's monologue through each passenger car. The mic checks began with spoken words, sometimes funny, often banal, and almost always ended with Johnny Cash or some other music we had deemed appropriate for our short run down to the ships. Later, our disembodied voices would tell the history of White Pass and the railroad, pointing out scenery, old bridges, flowers, and whatever wildlife wasn't spooked by the train.

On the way down to the docks from the staging area, some engineers used the air brakes, making for a somewhat softer ride, keeping the space between the cars constant so they wouldn't crash together. But others sped downhill, the cars rattling and banging together, throwing us around until we had bruises on our thighs. I got to know the passenger cars. Each had a different personality, a unique shape and design, and its own number or name. Some of the cars had much larger windows than others. Some had arched ceilings. Some had flowered carpet. Some had wide aisles that were easier to walk through. Some had twenty-six seats while others had forty.

But most mornings, I stood on an outside platform with a cup of coffee, the inevitable damp wind on my face. I would steady myself against the railing, swaying side-to-side with the movement of the car, putting one foot forward when the train slowed or stopped. I was outside for at least a few minutes, cherishing time to breathe, to notice which flowers were blooming, to be still and in motion at the same time. With no passengers on the train yet, I'd find myself in a place somewhere between meditation and the memory of being rocked to sleep, thinking about nothing at all. It took just ten minutes to get the trains down to the dock, but these were like the moments in a dream. It was this atypical synchronicity between man, machinery and nature that made me love the train. And when I think of Alaska today, those short trips are the first things that come to mind.

During an Alaskan summer, the light of 6 a.m. was the same as 10 p.m. No real sunrise and no real sunset. I recall sitting in front of the Golden North Hotel one night with a heavy glass mug of beer, admiring the alpenglow that dripped like Karo syrup across the tops of the numbered and mostly unnamed peaks surrounding the town. Alpenglow, not a sunset, but an almost liquid vibration, a reflection that occurred when the sun only just dipped behind the opposite horizon. Or perhaps it was a reminder of the constant, oblong, roller-coaster rotation of the earth around a hazy, understated sun that one only witnesses in the far North or South.

When people ask me about Alaska, they seem to want to hear about extremes. I saw and felt the opposite. I saw grayness there and learned to be content with it, to sit in it. Not only was the sky gray and the lakes laden with gray-blue glacial silt, but there existed a constant, never-changing cycle of things that would go unnoticed by those who weren't paying close attention. Seasons ran together like milk and coffee, a simultaneous and quiet darkening and lightening. Purple irises reluctantly reached toward the bright gray where the sun would have been, and we monitored their coming and going annually. The still, hanging clouds wouldn't budge, but were a steady wispy whitish horizontal line above our heads, obscuring the mountain tops and infuriating paying passengers. In the harbor, high tides climbed, hesitated with a breath, a pause, then retreated. The tails of a whale mother and her calf weaved over and under the water like the half-assed stitch I used to make a temporary repair in the cuff of my sleeve.

Cyclical, circular, the days and nights came together and spread apart like the air in the bellows of an accordion. I was keenly aware, yet focused softly without forcing myself to see. I didn't want to blink, but still made an effort to close my eyes because I knew that seeing was only part of the experience. I felt Alaska in my gut. I felt it on my skin. I still do.

I live in a condo on the north side of Denver, close to the freight train tracks. As I'm falling asleep at night, I can hear the long-long-short-long whistle that indicates a train is approaching an intersection. Two short whistles means the train is backing up. I learned these signals on the twenty miles of Alaskan track, traversed hundreds of times, befriending conductors who had worked for the railroad for thirty years or more, and finally getting permission from them to ride in the cabs of the sturdy old diesel engines. Inside, I was surrounded by a warm hum, feeling tall and able to see the tracks ahead, an impossible vantage point for any passenger car except one caboose, which had a highly coveted cupola.

The diesel engines were of two vintages. All smelled

of creosote and oil and fuel, and clicked sporadically while still. The newer, more powerful engines had square noses and loud smoking engines, while the 1950s versions were round in front, their idle higher pitched, quieter. The diesels did the day-to-day work, pulling as many as seventeen cars full of passengers to the summit of White Pass several times a day, three-and-a-half hours each way. As much as I admired these diesels, which were historic and masterfully restored, my favorite engine was a steamer, Number 73, which was only used for special tours and for showcasing around the depot. It was alive, breathing smoke, spewing steam; it had a throaty, gravelly idle.

Number 73 would plod diligently up the steep grade of the pass. The engineer tended to her every whim, gently adjusting gauges, constantly alert. It could pull four or five passenger cars, at most, and was challenging to drive. Too much steam and the boiler would burst, so the engineers maintained the right pressure by increasing the fire or releasing steam. I rode it to Lake Bennett once, and emerged speckled with oil, smiling. On that trip the engineer cooked sandwiches in foil on the firebox, and I pulled the whistle at some of the intersections. In the seasons that followed, I rode in that steam engine whenever I had the opportunity.

The history of the cars, the engines, and the route itself was overwhelming. It seemed impossible to absorb it all but I tried, even riding on my days off. I can put myself there, in the first few miles of tracks, whenever I like. I hear the whistling of metal on metal when the cars come around a bend, the rattle of the wheels over seams in the track, the fluctuations in the tone of the engine as we accelerate or slow down. From the deciduous trees along the river next to the tracks, to the famous cantilever bridge and tunnels, to the perfectly placed pick-axes and horse skulls near the summit, I can remember nearly every bit of track, and the way the flowers and clouds looked depending on the season. I couldn't imagine what the pass would have been like before the construction of the railroad. And to be honest, I didn't want to. The tracks and the trains seemed to belong there.

Balanced on narrow gauge tracks, the trains take essentially the same route as Klondike gold rush stampeders did, following the route of the White Pass Trail, which was advertised as an easier foot route than the more famous and more frequently documented Chilkoot trail. The Chilkoot started in Dyea, a neighboring town, now home to the previously mentioned irises and an old cemetery, but not much more. Dyea became a ghost town while Skagway survived because of the railroad, which was built to carry the men and women who had contracted gold fever. Unfortunately, the rush had ended before the railroad was completed. After that, the White Pass and Yukon route got people and things to and from Whitehorse, the capital of the Yukon, until the Skagway section of the Klondike Highway opened in 1978. The railroad shut down for a time, but reopened as a tourist attraction in the early 1980s.

I talked about these things on the tour. I talked about Soapy Smith, a con man who built bogus telegraph lines, collecting money from homesick stampeders whose messages never reached their intended recipients. I explained that the conical purplish-pink blossoms of fireweed that covered the hillsides of the highline bloomed from the bottom of the stalk to the top, finally releasing cottony spores to the wind in late summer. The tourists and I looked for mountain goats near the summit, and mourned the story about pack animals that, malnourished and overworked, plummeted to their deaths on the narrow portion of the trail now known as Dead Horse Gulch.

I took it upon myself to single-handedly portray the plight and the urgency of these determined men and women to modern-day tourists from Germany and Brooklyn, Iowa and Tokyo. I reminded my passengers that there was no such thing as Gore-Tex in the late 1800s, and that wool was heavy when wet and smelled terrible. Most were unconvinced, uninterested, or chose to focus on crumbs in the bottom of small bags of Lay's potato chips. Many heard little of the tour, instead pressing their faces against the glass, fervently searching for the bears that we almost never saw from the train. They couldn't envision it. They weren't rooted in it. They were anxious to get back to the ship in time for an early dinner. I can't blame them, really. A few hours is not enough to get a sense of a place.

I liked to fantasize about the hoards of people that came before us, before the tour guides and cruise ship passengers. When I walked the tracks behind the depot to the Dewey Lakes trailhead, I imagined the sound of heavy footsteps of horses and men, burdened with awkward packs of food, tools and camping gear who walked the same route a hundred years ago. When I looked down from the first overlook on the trail, I half expected to see dingy, dilapidated steamships at the docks instead of cruise liners. I wished to open my eyes and see battered black steam trains spewing sparks of coal and heavy ashes, vomiting deep, whining, hollow whistles that ricocheted against the rocky mountainside. So much had happened here, and I would have felt as if I were intruding if it weren't for the tourists, the shopkeepers, the tour guides— it really wasn't so different from the rush that happened just over a hundred years ago. The tourists come to Skagway, like the gold rushers did, looking for adventure and prestige. True, they stocked up on gold pans and wool clothing, while today the tourists haul home plastic bags of mugs, magnets, stuffed moose toys, and fleece shirts with "Alaska" embroidered on them. Skagway was, and still is, a thriving commercial hub. The ships, then as now, decimate the waters of the Inside Passage, carrying throngs of people from all over the world in their cold, steel bellies. Too many people invade the tiny town of Skagway, two miles long and a half-mile wide. They crawl along the boardwalks like angry ants stirred by a child's stick, stripping bare the shelves of souvenir shops. They stop in saloons for a drink. They complain about the inhospitable climate. They go to the store for groceries. They see what there is to see, and then they move on.

They go to Alaska—we have all gone to Alaska—to find adventure, to live out a dream, which for many is simply checking off Alaska a travel to-do list. But I have met a few who, like me, are afraid of the sharp peaks and asphyxiation-blue glaciers protruding from dark, almost frozen salt water. They somehow remember a time long before they existed, in a place they never lived—a memory stirred up by the shuffling of feet on elevated, creaking boardwalks and the distant jangle of a piano. They turn their faces toward a rain so light it nearly evaporates before seeping into and darkening the fabric of an overcoat. Alaska stirs something inside them, altering them forever. They vow to return to Alaska, and often they do. I know I will.

• • •

Melanie Colletti recently completed a Master's degree in Library and Information Science at the University of Denver and currently works as a clerk for the Denver Public Library, but she continues to daydream about Skagway and the train.

A Walk with Dinah

ANNIE TUPEK

Dinah's paws crunch through the snow, blotting out the tracks of smaller dogs. She walks at my side, nose to the ground, searching for scents. The snow isn't deep yet; it's early winter and unseasonably warm for November in Fairbanks. The temperatures hover in the upper teens, and while the sunlight is fast fading, the cloudless sky is a serene blue hue. Bare trunks of birch rise all around us, the leaves long fallen from the branches.

On this Saturday afternoon we could be alone in the world, walking a trail through Creamer's Field. I'm warm, bundled in the standard winter regalia of sub-Arctic Fairbanks: boots, parka, hat, gloves, scarf. Dinah sports leather booties to keep her paws from getting too weatherworn. She does not like them, but deals with them. The minute we get home she'll be trying to chew them off if I'm not fast enough for her liking.

She's a 150-pound English Mastiff, and her prints in the snow are almost as large as mine. This is one of our favorite places to take a walk; it's in the heart of Fairbanks, yet all to be heard in the boreal woods are chirping birds and the occasional creatures rustling through the undergrowth.

It's a popular place for dog walking, revealed by the mass of human and canine footprints marking the trail. There are all sorts of interesting smells for Dinah's nose and we meander slowly, enjoying the day and our quiet time together. Animal tracks parallel and cross the trail, disappearing into the cover of the trees.

I keep my eyes open for the well-camouflaged snowshoe hare. Brown in summer, their fur pales to white in autumn, and they are difficult to distinguish from their snowy surroundings. If Dinah catches sight of one, she's liable to knock me down in her excitement to give chase. She sniffs at the ground, finds the scent, and follows it into the trees.

She's on her retractable leash, which lets her wander

twenty feet from me, an illusion of freedom. Her tail is high and batting from side to side. I can hear the rapid sniff-sniff of her inhalations as she gets further from me. She's probably breathing in as much snow as scent. The nylon tape of her leash whisks against the brush, sending snow trickling to the ground, so soft it doesn't make a sound.

In this, the unfolding of winter, my thoughts return to the warm months, the endless summer days when the entire world is green and vibrant with life. When squirrels flick their tails and frolic through the trees, butterflies paint the air with their multitude of colors, the mosquitoes buzz and sting. I do not miss the mosquitoes.

This winter landscape, though snow-capped, is not dead. The life is hidden, resting, waiting for the midnight sun to return. Shrews tunnel under the snow; birds fluff up their feathers for warmth and stay close to their nests. There are probably a few moose in the area snacking on whatever succulents they can find, and a myriad of other creatures smart enough to stay out of the way of a human and her dog.

The leash tightens, the signal to Dinah that she

can go no further. She sighs, a heavy exhalation she must have learned from me, and returns to the trail. Disappointment fills her big brown eyes; snow covers her black muzzle, frosting it white. She shakes. The quaking beings at her head, her jowls flap and the snow goes flying. Her chain collar jingles and jangles, pealing through the silence of the woods. The wave ripples down her back; lock-kneed, her feet stomp the ground. The front half of her body already calmed, her tail flails from root to tip and then the shudder is gone.

It's a motion that never ceases to make me laugh. Her baleful eyes turn to me, wondering what it is that I find amusing—certainly not her. I pat her head and tell her she's a good girl. She wags her tail.

We've been in one place for too long. Dinah has exhausted the interest out of the scents, as I won't let her go further into the trees. We move down the trail. Out of the woods, we walk between broad fields. Headlights of cars traveling down College Road are visible in the distance, and the other worldliness of the woods is gone. The sound of the mild traffic doesn't reach this far, but the lights flickering through the sparse trees lining the road maintain a magical effect.

Creamer's Field is two thousand acres of fields, wetlands, and forest. Its official designation as Creamer's Field Migratory Waterfowl Refuge is a bit of a mouthful, so Fairbanksans call it Creamer's Field, or even just Creamer's. Originally a 250-acre dairy farm founded by Charles and Belle Hinckley in 1904, it was purchased by Charles and Anna Creamer in 1928. It was once interior Alaska's most successful dairy farm, but when modern shipping made it no longer profitable to run, it was closed down and the land was put up for sale. Townspeople banded together and, with the help from the state and other charitable donations and organizations, purchased the land in 1966. Additional parcels of land were added over the years, bringing it to its current size. These caring residents created a non-profit organization that hosts nature and wildlife events year round.

The fields that Dinah and I walk through are the summer breeding grounds for several thousand Sandhill cranes. Before the snow fully melts in the springtime, volunteers will strew the ground with barley seed. When the cranes arrive, along with the other migrant species that call Alaska home for the summer, they will feast on the seed sprouts. Some cranes continue farther north, but many stay throughout the summer.

In late August, the Sandhill Crane Festival marks the beginning of their migration back to Texas. Birdwatching stations are set up on the perimeter of the fields, along with arts and crafts booths. It's a major fundraising event; local artists and businesses donate items for auction to benefit the Refuge. I bid on a Sandhill crane drawing at last year's silent auction, but was outbid. Still, Dinah and I had a fun time that day, too.

Leashed dogs are allowed when the cranes are in residence, but the fields are off-limits and everyone must stay to the trails. Dinah loves the cranes; I think it's because of their astounding six-foot-plus wingspan. They're one of the few birds that can look larger than her. Long, lean legs support an ovoid body; a streamlined head and beak sit atop a long, lean neck. Under the mud stains, their feathers are gray. Their most distinguishing characteristic, apart from size and silhouette, is the scarlet red that caps the top half of their heads. They can fly up to four hundred miles in one day from warmer, southern climates—but not to be a meal for a dog. During our summertime walks through

Creamer's Field, Dinah is confined to her short leash.

She is unappreciative of this security measure. Her soft eyes ask, beg, to be let loose, to run free and frolic with the dancing cranes. I must make my heart hard and deny her request. When the cranes call to each other with their extensive vocabulary, Dinah chimes in with a soft bark of her own. It cannot be mistaken for the cranes' throaty, rattling trills that end with a short squawk, and the birds, knowing they're safe, ignore her and dance.

Pairs, believed to be mated for life, bow to each other and hop. They spread their wings wide; the feathers on the tips separate to look like fingers. They flap their wings and kick their feet, dip their heads to the ground and fling sticks up into the air. A dramatic ballet, it is thought to serve as both a mating ritual and as a teaching tool to instruct young cranes, called colts.

They are very social animals and among the oldest species of birds, as evidenced by a ten-million-year-old fossil from Nebraska whose structure is identical to modern Sandhill cranes. The family groups migrate together; the ones that visit Fairbanks are of the mid-continent population of Lesser Sandhill Cranes.

Creamer's Field is also home to the Alaska Bird Observatory, the northernmost research station of its kind in North America. The scientists there primarily study population trends in migrating songbirds. They band the birds and release them into the wild unharmed. The data collected by the ornithologists and their many volunteers has been invaluable in assessing threats to avian populations and protecting habitats. They also assist in producing wildlife management guidelines and have extensive educational programs.

Dinah and I are reaching the end of the trail. The structures of Creamer's Field are close by to the right. The façade of the old farmhouse, formerly the residence of the Creamer family and now the visitor center, is two stories tall, with white siding and black trim. With the snow, it seems to blend in with the surrounding fields. The barns still stand, one of them announcing "Creamer's Dairy" in massive letters on its sloped roof. As the snow thickens, the letters will be obscured. The Friends of Creamer's Field are currently working to make these larger outbuildings open for public viewing.

The cozy, small rooms of the visitor's center are

filled with displays of wildlife and the history of the Refuge. This is a community place, and knowledgeable volunteers lead nature walks and staff the center. They are always enthusiastic to answer questions and share information with the flocks of bird-watchers who descend on the Refuge during the summer.

Peering through binoculars, the bird-watchers spot golden plovers and mallards, warblers and swallows along with the Sandhill Cranes. Guides and checklists close at hand, they whisper together excitedly. Occasionally one will make a loud announcement and point to the skies: "A northern harrier! Look!" A faint dark blur circles high above the treetops. Binoculars are raised, guidebooks consulted, and checklists marked. Their enthusiasm is contagious. Dinah senses the excitement and makes quick side steps, eyes on the cranes in the field, unconcerned with the birds overhead.

The midnight sun is long gone, and so are the cranes. All but the most hardcore bird-watchers are snug in their homes, watching the birdfeeders outside their windows. Here at Creamer's, the fields are blanketed by snow; the traces of the summer residents decompose and are reincorporated into the soil. Come spring breakup there will be no evidence of the cranes until their return.

We pass through the open gate, leaving the snowy trail for the icy sidewalk. I unzip my parka and loosen my scarf. Dinah and I continue our walk, past the farmhouse and to the car. Summer will return, along with the cranes. But until then, we wait.

• • •

Annie Tupek was born and raised in the suburbs of Chicago. She now resides in Fairbanks with her husband and their adopted English Mastiff. Her short work has appeared in *The First Line* magazine (Spring, 2007) and the forthcoming horror anthology *Courting Morpheus* (Belfire Press, January 2010). As a buyer and office assistant at Gulliver's Books, America's northernmost independent bookstore, her reading addiction is well sated, though she often despairs that there are too many books and not enough time for reading.

The Hunt

JOHN M. LIBAL

Moose hunting, when done properly, affords an individual with a great deal of time for contemplation. One would be hard-pressed to find longtime Alaskan hunters who base the success of their outdoor experience on solely killing game. No, hunting in the wilderness up here exposes one to a stage much grander than that. One day's events during a recent seven-day hunt bring that truth home.

Awakened by my internal alarm clock, I open my eyes to a dark, cold cabin; morning's light is still an hour away. After reveling in the warmth of my sleeping bag for a few more minutes, emitting a half grunt, half groan, I launch myself from one of the top bunks. Bottom bunks are reserved for camp elders, and even nearing forty years of age, I shoehorned my way onto the top bunk last night, as I am still considered a boy in this hunting camp. Quickly dressing while listening to a sprinkling patter of an early September rain on the roof, I open the cabin door, steeling myself for a soggy trek to the makeshift outhouse.

I hurriedly return to take part in an early morning ballet with the four other members of our hunting party. Sleepily pulling on damp camouflage and other hunting apparel, we look like a group of grizzled models preparing for a *Cabela's* catalog shoot. We head out and split up for destinations frequented by moose in the morning.

Nothing attracts my attention as I work my way through a stand of Sitka spruce and settle in to watch the hillside view. I've chosen a tree known for its natural gun-rest, from which several bull moose have been shot. Although it doesn't provide the expansive view of other areas, the small valley bisecting this part of my hunting territory is a known thoroughfare for rutting moose.

After many years of hunting on the Kenai Peninsula in south central Alaska, I know what most experienced seekers of moose know: with the combination of Alaska's shortened daylight hours in the fall, a wide variety of inclement weather, dense brush, a moose's acute hearing, and its inexplicable ability to move its half-ton body stealthily through the brush, it is a formidable and challenging game animal, making any hunter very lucky just to get a chance for a shot.

Consequently, it is not surprising that many of my mornings mimic the experiences of most moose hunters. The sun rises uneventfully despite a few suspicious sounds: a branch breaking, a muffled grunt, and a leafy belch. It's times like these when I find myself hoping to hear nearby shots announcing the success of another member of my group. Unfortunately, that does not occur this morning either, and after three hours, I pack my gear, sling my rifle, and return to the cabin to enjoy a hot breakfast of pancakes and sausage.

Later, my father and I make our way along another worn trail through the orange, yellow and brown-mottled willows to the Overlook. My father is not young anymore, and we must take time and care during the half-mile junket from camp. Although movement isn't as easy for him as it once was, like the other camp elders, he still looks forward to the annual ten-mile, four-wheeler drive to hunting camp, a trip most folks his age would consider inconvenient at best, at worse dangerous.

Yet this is a common practice for many aging Alaskans. Having entered the forty-ninth state when it was still called the Last Frontier, these individuals are accustomed to the challenges that need to be overcome when enjoying its wilderness; many continue to be active well into the years that find others their age in nursing homes. And they bring along their children and grandchildren, encouraging them to experience the Alaska that lured them here and still holds them fast.

The Overlook gets its name because it sits on the edge of a hill that commands an impressive view of much of the Caribou Hills (although a majority of the caribou roaming the Kenai Peninsula died off after a major forest fire in the early 1900s and caribou are rarely seen in the area). In the distance to the west are the Ninilchik Domes, and dominating the skyline to the north is Hill 26. These two promontories form the bookends of a ten-square-mile area of grayish-brown beetle-killed spruce, brilliant, gold-leafed cottonwood trees, dense willows, and alders. Completing the patch-work taiga are hillsides scattered with fields of magen-ta fireweed and large muskegs pock-marked by small lakes and waterholes where the first tendrils of Anchor River and Deep Creek begin to flow.

As my father and I scan the usual haunts for moose, the afternoon silence is interrupted by the cacophonous calls of an approaching flock of Sandhill Cranes. At first their formation bears a greater resemblance to smoke-like haze on the horizon than actual birds in flight, but soon, nearly three hundred cranes create an undulating V-Shaped, feathered filament "cree-crawing" its way across the sky. Catching an updraft, the cranes circle in a spiraling sphere, gaining necessary altitude before continuing their ancient journey south over the Kenai Mountains. And ... just like that ... it is silent again.

The appearance of the cranes is a long-awaited sig-nal that the moose rut is beginning. During the rut, bull moose lose their inhibitions, making them par-ticularly susceptible to the alluring sounds of another moose rubbing his antlers on brush, sounds deceptively duplicated by hunters using an old moose scapula or even an empty oil can.

Yet the migration of the cranes marks much more to many Alaskans. Their cries announce that another spring and summer have passed: an end to the family communion of fishing for king salmon and halibut on the waters of lower Cook Inlet; memories of picking blueberries and crowberries on hillsides shared with brown and black bears; harvest time for gardeners whose bounty was made large in the long summer hours of the Land of the Midnight Sun. The cries bespeak of the approach of winter, holding Alaska and its citizens in its frozen, darkened, six-month grasp. The silence left after the cranes' departure gives birth to a season of remembrance.

This, and much more, passes through my mind while at the Overlook. As moose are not as likely to be moving during the daytime hours, the time spent there is often perfunctory from a practical hunting aspect. However, my father and I use this time to discuss other issues: the health of the family, how work is going, and upcoming plans for the winter. Seated on chairs, glassing the hillsides and muskegs with binoculars, we pass our time between contemplation and conversation. Dad smokes his favorite pipe, while I enjoy the waning heat of the fall sun peaking through the clouds overhead. As with the morning hunt, no moose make their appearance in the afternoon. With a tinge of disappointment, and slight concern that the moose have still not shown in great numbers, we return to camp to relate the story of our sightings, or lack thereof.

The remainder of the afternoon is consumed by a session of fireside hunting stories capped off by a meal of fried potatoes and rib-eye steaks. After dinner, as in the afternoon, my father and I decide to spend the evening hunt together. Repeating an age-old ritual, we don our hunting gear, sling our rifles over our shoulders, and make our way along a brush-lined trail to a vantage called the Point, a sparsely treed knob that looks down on another muskeg often frequented by moose. Once set up in position, we sit patiently, watching both the muskeg and two small valleys forming arms on either side of the point.

Around eight o'clock, the sun drops behind the mountains that bridge the gap between Iliamna and Redoubt volcanoes in the west, turning the new snow on the high peaks pink with the fading daylight. A high plume of steam climbs from Redoubt's main cone, proof that the volcano has yet to return to slumber after its massive eruptions in March and April. For moose hunters, the time between sunset and dusk is often the most fruitful. Called the witching hour by many, this is a time when the day breeze from nearby Kachemak Bay diminishes, making it easier to hear. Of course, just as hunters can hear more easily, so too can the moose, so our conversation dies to a whisper. This time also marks when the animals begin to stir from their afternoon beds for their nightly search of food and water, and it's not long before Dad breaks the silence with a quiet whistle of alert. In hushed tones he excitedly exclaims what all hunting partners love to hear.

"There's a moose!"

We immediately raise our binoculars to determine the gender of our quarry. After a short pause, we confirm it.

"It's a cow."

Still, we remain attentive to the cow's behavior. Although mainly solitary for most of the season, during the rut, many moose act like herd animals. If the cow were to look behind her into the brush, it is likely that she is being followed by another animal. More often than not, that animal will be another cow or calf, but as the number of cows in the herd multiplies, the chance that one or more bulls will be in their company increases significantly.

This evening, the cow seems to be alone and is moving fast. Even at three hundred yards, the rasp of her panting breath can be easily heard. Her ability to quickly move through the difficult terrain of grassy hummocks and snarls of willow brush means she will only be in view for a minute. It would take a hunter more than twenty times that to cover the same amount of ground. Double-checking her head for horns, we mutually agree as she disappears.

"It was definitely a cow."

As the twilight dwindles to darkness, it's time to call it a night. Even if we were to see a bull moose now, it would be impossible for us to determine if it had a legal antler width or the right number of brow tines. As we return to camp, our hushed conversation is infused with a noticeable degree of excitement. The cow was heading somewhere; we can only hope it was in search of a nearby bull.

After relating our story to the other members of the hunting party, and listening to the different versions of the other's adventures, it is time to hit the sack. Climbing into the top bunk for the night, I consider the possibilities of the next day. As with most nights in the cabin—void of the click and hum of electronic gadgetry known in my everyday life—I drift off quickly. The last thing I hear before entering my dreams is the snoring of well-seasoned elders who know when it's time to sleep.

There are many lessons of life to be learned while hunting and living in Alaska: the importance of passing-on the experience of elders; the awe-inspiring, rugged and beautiful wilderness; an appreciation for a natural harvest provided from its land and waters; reflections of how it changes people as time passes; and the enjoyment of time spent with parents, children and friends. These are the underlying ideals upon which survival in Alaska has been founded, ideals valued by those residents who are willing to accept the harshness of the extended winter for the offerings of the other seasons.

Alaska's wilderness has been described as a playground and an unforgiving mistress, where the most innocent adventure can instantaneously become a matter of survival; where it is not uncommon to walk your dog while armed with a pistol for fear of bear attack; where an afternoon outing on the water can turn into a hypothermic plunge and a frantic swim for shore. These disparate juxtapositions provide an excellent arena for adventurers to test their mettle.

Indeed, much of Alaska is populated by these adventurers who came for various reasons: to make their fortune, put down new roots, escape hardship, or live a more simplified life. Many never find what they were originally looking for, but most stay because of what they do discover, both in the land and in themselves.

• • •

John M. Libal worked for several years at Title Wave Books in Anchorage, which is still managed by his wife, Angela, and now approaching twenty years in business. He currently works at Everts Air Cargo at the Anchorage International Airport.

IDAHO

STATE MOTTO "Esto perpetua" ("It is forever")

STATE SONG "Here We Have Idaho"

STATE TREE Western white pine

STATE HORSE Appaloosa

STATE FISH Cutthroat trout

STATE FOSSIL Hagerman Horse fossil

STATE FRUIT Wild huckleberry

STATE TRIVIA:

• Hell's Canyon is the deepest gorge in America, deeper than the Grand Canyon.

• 465 river miles from the ocean, Lewiston is the Pacific's farthest inland seaport.

• 63% of Idaho is public land managed by the federal government.

• In 1955, Arco became the first city in the world to have its electricity generated by nuclear reactor.

• Idaho was possibly named as the result of a hoax, sometimes referred to as the "Idahoax." In the early

1860s, when the United States Congress was considering organizing a new territory in the Rocky Mountains, eccentric lobbyist George M. Willing suggested the name "Idaho," which he claimed was derived from a Shoshone term meaning "the sun comes from the mountains" or "gem of the mountains." Willing later admitted that he made up the name. Congress ultimately decided to name the area Colorado Territory; however, "Idaho" did not go away. The same year Congress created Colorado Territory, a new county in eastern Washington Territory was named Idaho County, after a steamship that was launched on the Columbia River. Idaho County became the Idaho Territory and, eventually, the state of Idaho.

• Famous Idahoans: Ernest Hemingway, Harmon Killebrew, Paul Revere (and the Raiders), Picabo Street, Chief Joseph, Sarah Palin, Patrick McManus, Philo T. Farnsworth (inventor of television), Sacagawea, Ted Trueblood

Blue Eden

MARCIA VANDERFORD

I see it every day, the breathtakingly beautiful and sparkling blue of Lake Pend Oreille. Eons ago, glaciers scraped out its depths, and dramatic mountains rose up to ring its shores, towering peaks that poke the azure of the north Idaho sky. Its hundred miles of shoreline have been the landscape of my life for as long as I can remember.

On the lake, perched just beyond a large sandy peninsula, is the small resort town of Sandpoint. Sitting in the panhandle of Idaho, we are sixty miles from the Canadian border and just twenty miles each way to Washington and Montana. The town was established at the turn of the twentieth century when the railroad came through, bringing farmers, loggers, and miners.

Ferry boats provided transportation across the water. Merchants set up shop to serve the populace, which, by all accounts, was a wild and wooly bunch. A Spanish Mission style theater built to accommodate traveling troupes of all kinds has been beautifully restored and is still in use for its original purpose, albeit to tamer audiences.

By the 1950s, Sandpoint was a logging and farming community with a population of just three thousand, and things had calmed down considerably from those earlier times. No one thought anything of leaving the house with just the screen door shut, no locks. We passed in and out of the neighborhood homes freely, played with communal pets, and visited with that nice old couple across the street who always seemed glad to see us. We roller-skated down bumpy streets, acquiring scraped knees and bruises. It was six blocks to downtown, and we could explore it on our own. The five-and-dime store was popular for the goldfish and canaries, and sometimes we would sneak a spritz of the exotic Evening of Paris perfume. On Saturday afternoon, we would congregate at the then-rundown Panida Theater to watch second-run movies for the exorbitant price of one quarter. We would amble home for dinner, always served at the same time. Our parents took for granted that we would appear when expected.

As a child, I had no notion that I lived in a sort of Eden, the lake at the center of our paradise. One of my earliest memories is of lying on my back in the cool water, bobbing on top of the rippling surface of the lake. My father, a former lifeguard and college athlete, is giving me a little push, first one direction and then another. "You float like a cork!" he proudly exclaims.

With every passing school year, the lake continued to lure us to its shores every summer. Of course, many of us had been wading in its frigid snowmelt-fed waters since April. We would throw off our shoes and jackets with abandon and jump right in, the seagulls wheeling overhead. Our hair whipped across our faces in the wind, and we screamed our joy to the world. I still recall that feeling of wild exaltation.

That joy had to be earned. Swimming lessons were mandatory for any child living near such a wild, deep, and unpredictable body of water. Wind could kick up three-foot waves, and our parents made sure that we all could help ourselves if caught out on the water. We walked down to the city beach several times a week, rain or shine, at some ungodly hour in the morning to take lessons from the newly minted instructors, high school students who had just completed the life-saving course. This went on every summer for two to three years until we practically grew gills.

We spent family summers in our old catamaran speedboat, seven feet across the bow and almost impossible to sink. With my father as captain, my mother in the "slow down, Richard" position, and my older brother and me taking up the rear, we would pack our lunch and head out for the day. We would take a tour of the many little bays and islands, often stopping to explore the woods and skip stones. After arguments about the most skips, and some arm-punching from my brother, my dad would break things up by asking, "How about some water-skiing?"

Usually we would start skiing from the shore of one of the little islands in the lake. Now the islands are all too developed with multi-million-dollar homes, fancy docks, and KEEP OUT signs, but back then there might have been the odd cabin where a local family came to spend the weekends. For the most part, the islands were deserted. Life jackets on, we would wrestle the unwieldy water skis onto our feet while trying to keep ourselves from tilting sideways. Rope between bent knees, treading water until there was tension in the line, and then "Hit it!" Lean forward, oops, too far, face plant. Eventually, each of us managed to rise out of the depths, and once we did, it was like flying. The skis cut a line through the waves and the boat wake, and we'd wave triumphantly to family in the boat, grinning like idiots.

In the water, on the water, near the water. Eden.

Alas, growing up in such a small place can be stifling over time, so after graduating from high school, I went off to college and the wider world, vowing never to return. I did stay away for several years, returning only for school vacations and, of course, summer at the lake. Cities have their charms, as do drier climes, but they never felt like home to me. Several years later, I returned home full-time to work and raise my family. Sandpoint had changed quite a bit in my short time away, having been discovered by the rest of the country, but the essence of the place still remained, the blues of the lake at its core. It's why others were coming to my town.

Our children have all gone to pursue their dreams, but we are still here at the water's edge and still love to get out on the lake. A lifelong friend recently acquired and renovated a double-decker houseboat, and she, my husband, and I sneak away from the daily routine as often as possible. We load up the boat and leisurely coast along the shore, soaking up the sun and breeze. No phone and no electronic distractions. We sip our drinks and critique the various architectural projects we pass by.

Then we strike out across the big lake towards the majestic Green Monarch Mountains that plunge straight down into the water. At some point, we crank up the music of our youth and sing badly at the top of our lungs. There's no one there to hear us, usually. We stop the boat in the middle of that vast blue expanse and take a flying leap into its welcoming, watery arms. We are refreshed, and in some ways we are restored to that glorious state where adult worries are chased away.

In the cold clear water, we do not feel any particular age. We are at one with our own particular universe, our blue Eden.

• • •

Marcia Vanderford and her husband, Tom, own Vanderford's Books & Office Products in Sandpoint. They have hosted many local and national authors at the store in their thirty years in business. They are both Idaho natives, have three grown sons, and feel privileged to have the beauty of north Idaho just steps from their back door.

The Spirit of Idaho

JUDITH R. LOHREY WUTZKE

To me, Idaho means warm kitchens and history books, small farms and smaller schools, rural life but a bigger world all around. It means a spirit of both self-reliance and community that saw me through childhood and into adulthood, and nourishes me still.

Along with her parents and ten siblings, my mother moved from Arkansas to a farm in central Idaho, attended high school for a few years, and later earned her GED. When World War II started, she joined the WAVES and was stationed in Rhode Island, where she worked in a traffic control tower. After the war, she returned to Clearwater, married my dad, and later became county assessor.

My father's family moved to central Idaho in the

1920s. My dad had a fourth-grade education and spent his life working hard as a tree hooker in the woods and later as a crew boss for the Forest Service. He had no desire to travel any further than the next town, and then only on Saturdays.

Our mom had a broader vision and wanted more for her three children. Mother knew her knowledge and skills were limited in some areas, so when we wanted to study a subject, Mom would find someone to teach us. We went to the Good News after-school club on Wednesdays taught by Maude Breen, who raised her family of seven by herself and was an example of love and laughter in spite of great adversity. Along the way, I learned how to cook, can, and freeze our food. I learned about the wildflowers, trees, and geology of the area and traveled all around Idaho on field trips. When one of my teachers told the girls that we didn't need math because we were just going to get married, I took my mother's advice and took as many business courses as possible. Most importantly, Mom said there was always someone worse off than we were, and we'd better figure out how to help them.

•

Our first home was the old doctor's house, built in the 1800s. The front door opened onto the boardwalk in town—yes, a boardwalk, just like in movies of the Old West. That's what Clearwater was like in the late 1940s. When I was six months old, that house burned to the ground, along with another house and the Baptist church. The community joined together and built us a three-room home, and also rebuilt the church. The new house had no indoor bathroom, and the only hot water we had was heated on the top of the stove, but we loved it. Soon after, we welcomed a baby girl to the family, and when I was eight years old, we moved into a house with an indoor bathroom and hot water from the faucet.

We were among the poorest citizens of central Idaho when measured by worldly goods, but we were blessed with riches in other ways. One of them was growing up near loving grandparents. My dad's father was night watchman at the lumber mill above town. Grandpa rode his horse to and from work, and on weekends, he stopped at our home and my older brother and I rode on the back of his horse, Ole Darby, while he walked alongside. We spent many Saturdays with Grandpa and

Grandma Lohrey helping grind horseradish, clean cabbage for coleslaw, feed the chickens, and gather eggs.

I have wonderful memories of a loving, lively household, one of which is the sight and fragrance of maple bars as they came out of our oven. Another that brings a smile to my face is of my father claiming my mother should be able to can and freeze all of the bounty he brought her from his huge garden after she worked a long week at her job. One day she reached her breaking point, and when Dad brought in yet another armful of produce, she chased him outside and told him he could just plow up the rest of the garden for all she cared. We also learned never to touch the TV dial when wrestling was on because Dad would swat us across the rear. I talked on the phone with girlfriends every evening, and my Dad would say, "Now, Judi, get off that phone; quit talking and get-a-goin'." My brother still ends our phone conversations with, "Judi, you'd better get-a-goin'."

Summers in a small town near the Bitterroots seemed to go on forever, but I was saved from boredom by the Bookmobile. That van was full of books that I could have for two weeks, and they took me to any place in the world my heart desired. I checked out the maximum number of books and spent many nights reading long after the rest of the family was asleep—the start of a lifelong attachment to the written word that later became my vocation.

Clearwater was a strong community. Everyone cried together when tragedy occurred and laughed together at weddings and at country dances held at the Grange and Odd Fellow halls. Only after supper was served at midnight did we go home. Now, many years later, we still gather in these same buildings as adults, both those who no longer live in the area and those who remained, as a group called the Clearwater Kids. People return from all over the country to renew friendships and raise money to support the EMTs and volunteer fire department or to preserve landmark buildings.

I was happily volunteering with various organizations in the area when I learned my favorite bookstore was being sold. The owner couldn't find a buyer so she decided that she would close the store, but she first asked if we were interested. My husband, Gary, said that I had finally gone off the deep end, but I calmly showed him how we could find the financing to buy the store, and he agreed. Now I am enjoying a second career as a business owner of ...and BOOKS, too!, the very best business for me. My brother's history books are on the shelf, and my customers are lifelong friends as well as newcomers and visitors. I can still be an important contributor to the state that has nurtured me my entire life—a state filled with good books, warm food, schools and meeting places, and, yes, Idaho spirit.

• • •

Judith R. Lohrey Wutzke is the owner of ...and BOOKS, too! in Lewiston, Idaho, and loves to read mysteries, general fiction, and local history books.

OREGON

STATE NICKNAME Beaver State

STATE MOTTO "She flies with her own wings"

STATE SONG "Oregon, My Oregon"

STATE FLOWER Oregon grape

STATE FISH Chinook salmon

STATE TREE Douglas fir

STATE SHELL Oregon hairy triton

STATE MUSHROOM Pacific golden chanterelle

STATE NUT Hazlenut (Oregon is the only state that has an official state nut. The hazelnut is also known as the filbert.)

STATE TRIVIA:

- Oregon has more ghost towns than any other state.
- Crater Lake is the deepest lake in the U.S.
- Sea Lion Caves is the largest sea cave in the world.
- Oregon is one of only two states without self-serve gas. (New Jersey is the other.)

• The first and only aerial bombing of mainland America by a foreign power occurred on September 9, 1942 when a Japanese seaplane launched from a submarine attempted to start a forest fire by dropping two incendiary bombs near Brookings, Oregon. No significant damage was reported following the attack, nor after a repeat attempt on September 29.

• The world's largest hairball resides at the Mt. Angel Abbey and Seminary. It was discovered in an Oregon City meatpacking plant in the late 1950s, cut from the belly of a 300-pound swine. Weighing in at two-and-one-half pounds, the calcified, gut-polished lump of hog bristle and plaque is considered the heftiest known hairball in the world. (Special thanks to Chuck Palahniuk for this tidbit.)

• Famous Oregonians: James Beard, Matt Groening, Ursula LeGuin, Ken Kesey, Linus Pauling, Abigail Scott Duniway, Beverly Cleary, Chuck Palahniuk, Gus Van Sant, Phil Knight, William Stafford, Steve Prefontaine

Finding Bayocean

GIGI LITTLE

Never mind that I moved to Oregon to find true love in a man I hardly knew. Who I'd only met through e-mail. Who was probably gay. Not to mention the whole thing about me running away from the circus. That stuff is incidental to the way I love this place. Or maybe it's not.

I'm the kind of perpetual tourist that comes from having spent fifteen years seeing the country—but not seeing it. Most of what I saw of America was the inside of a tent. On days off from the circus, we'd hit the road to watch another circus. I was married to a man who lived and loved, worked and played, talked and thought nothing but circus. I tried to adapt. If I couldn't see Mount Rushmore or Colonial Williamsburg, by god I was going to be happy taking a blurry picture of some historical marker from our moving car. In order to fill the great need for that something else in life, I became desperately fascinated with anything new I could lay my eyes on. Or wrap my heart around. To this day, I'm still a fascinated person. Back then I was just desperate.

In 2003 I took a trip—not a circus trip, just a me trip—to Portland, where I saw an art exhibit. The artist painted himself in 1930s Hollywood gowns. This seemed brave and strangely sexy. I sent him an e-mail fan letter, which turned into a year's correspondence, which turned into a decision to change everything.

Oddly, in all my fifteen years losing my pants across the country—which is to say I was a clown—I never played Oregon. There was something comforting in this as I packed to leave my then-husband in autumn 2004, as if the Portland rains could wash away every last clinging whiff of cotton candy and elephant urine. And my old life.

And as my plane dipped down out of a white thick of cloud and started its descent into Portland that day, there they were: sudden great marbles of water that tick-tick-ticked and broke in pieces like mercury against my airplane window.

I couldn't see the famous volcanic peak, Mount Hood, through the rain, but I didn't care. I raised my glass—a Shirley Temple because I was too cheap to spring for the booze—and toasted freedom and adventure.

When I was settling in, getting to know this man, we walked all over Portland. Past brewpubs and coffee houses. Almost every business was independent. The manhole covers were embossed with roses, and the sidewalks were mottled green with moss. Dog walkers and bicycles everywhere.

"That's Skidmore Fountain," Stephen would say. "Those little troughs on the bottom were designed for dogs. I guess for its dedication, Henry Weinhard offered to pump beer through it."

"That's Chapman School. See the smoke stack? In September, thousands of swifts nest in there."

I loved it all. Portland wasn't an endless skyscraper city or a wide-open tumbleweeds-and-bars city. Just the perfect kind of Goldilocks just-right. It even had its own smell. Something sweet and real. Coffee and roses and wet dog.

Then the wind would change, would run past the breweries, and what I would smell was beer. Good artisan Portland beer.

We walked past the Multnomah County Courthouse where, only six months before, clerks had issued marriages to same-sex couples. It only lasted forty-nine days, but in the big picture of civil rights, this was a great step forward. I was ecstatic to be in this historic place, looking for love with a man I'd first seen on an art gallery wall, posed in a dress.

The painting-himself-in-dresses thing and the pretty-gay-but-also-according-to-him-somewhat-straight thing was part of the appeal. This was me we were talking about. I'd married a makeup-wearing, ruffle-clad circus performer, for god's sake. Now I'd left that clown and moved to Portland: home of Gus Van Sant, Chuck Palahniuk, Pink Martini, the Dada Ball, and Darcelle XV, the oldest drag club in the country.

It was also the most vegetarian-friendly city in the country. And the most green-friendly. It was also the city whose hub was a four-story independent bookstore with more than a million titles, a rare book room, its own art gallery—oh dear god, this was it. I had to work at Powell's City of Books.

Instead I was hired at a gelato shop across the street—with an Italian name, an American owner and a Romanian chef who shouted at us from the back room. He emoted in half-hour-long rants as we were trying to clean up at night: "Always you girls do everything wrong. Oh, my heart is broken for this job."

The part of me not so easily humiliated kind of liked the job. Afternoons full of tiny tastes of gem-colored sorbetto; the rich, deep smell of espresso; and the opportunity to learn that the singular form of panini is panino. Portland was a little hunk of Europe on the west edge of the United States. It wasn't just me going all romantic over my gelato. People call it the best European city in America.

Thing is, Portland is different from much of Oregon—something that surprised me as I was getting to know the state better. In fact, Oregon is one of the most politically polarized states in the union. Look at the map. The Willamette Valley in the northwest, including Portland, Salem, and Eugene, is blue surrounded by red—a little blue bleeding over to the coast. Ashland, home of the Oregon Shakespeare Festival, is a dot of blue in the red of the southern counties. Hop over the Cascades, where central and eastern Oregon, with their ranchlands and farmlands, are all red with maybe a splotch of blue at Bend. But more interesting: the liberal areas are some of the most liberal in the country, and the conservative areas, some of the most conservative. Makes for a colorful mix of policies. We've got one of the nation's lowest effective state tax rates but also an assisted suicide law. We've decriminalized marijuana but also have few restrictions on carrying guns, even machine guns.

Oregon's always been at odds with itself. Settlers against Native Americans. Loggers against environmentalists. Cows against sheep. At the turn of the last century, central and eastern Oregon were all open range. Share and share alike. Which usually leads to war—this one between cattlemen and sheepmen, with the cattlemen organizing vigilante groups, such as the Crook County Sheep-Shooters Association, and killing thousands of sheep. There's still hostility between different factions of Oregonians—the city folk, the ranchers, the loggers—but now the wars are played out in gossip. "Yeah, the loggers are the twisted ones," my friend Chris says. And does a little air-banjo *Deliverance* riff.

Oregon is also very white. In the 1920s, we reportedly had the largest concentration of Ku Klux Klan outside the Deep South. Because the black population was so small, the Klan mostly focused their efforts on freeing the land of Catholics.

Back in 1844, before we were even a state, the Provincial Government of Oregon made two decrees: that the slaves were free, and that each black person would be whipped every six months "until he or she shall quit the territory."

The penalty was reduced to hard labor, but Oregon's KEEP OUT sign stayed up. The original state constitution barred blacks, Asians and Native Americans—they lumped Latinos in there, too—from owning land or voting. Native Americans were set on reservations; then with the United States' Termination Policy of 1953, many tribes were dissolved. Japanese-Americans were stuck in internment camps during World War II. And as for those forty-nine days of same-sex marriage in Portland: we now have a new prejudice written into the state constitution, defining marriage as one man/ one woman.

Sometimes making strides in the world is like salmon leaping up waterfalls.

This perpetual tourist would rather think about other things Oregon takes to extremes. We have everything: volcanic mountains, coastal rainforest, eastern desert. We have the nation's deepest lake (Crater Lake) and the world's shortest river (so short they just named it D). We have lava tubes, waterfalls, wetlands, a salt lake (Abert), buttes made of obsidian, a mountain named Three Fingered Jack, and claim to the largest single organism in the world, an *Armillaria ostoyae* fungus (honey mushroom) stretching 3.5 miles under eastern Oregon's Malheur National Forest. Take that, Loch Ness Monster.

And, for celebrating your thirty-seventh birthday with your pretty-gay-but-also-somewhat-straight boyfriend, we have what some say is the greatest coast, with sandy beaches right up against old growth forest and three separate sea monoliths all called Haystack Rock.

Summer, 2005. I had my face in the passenger window the entire drive to the ocean. I was having two love affairs, of course. This man and this place. In a way, Stephen was like Oregon to me. Oh, he'd never wear flip-flops in the rain, but he was the same kind of new and fresh and exciting. Stephen in the shower was the Portland Opera. Stephen in the kitchen was lush Oregon goat cheese and hazelnuts and lovely local pinot noir. Stephen in jeans painting himself in dresses was Oregon's polarity, its diversity, its unbending drive to express itself.

We stayed at a friend's beach house in Bay City, upper mid-coast, above Tillamook, which is famous for cheese. Nothing is more sensual, food-wise, than cheese, so we started there, at a place called the Blue Heron Cheese and Wine Company. The tasting was like a buffet in a gift shop, where you helped yourself to eraser-sized slices and dipped pretzels in various types of goo. Instead we went to the counter and ordered cheese plates and wine and had our own tasting—of surprisingly basic cheese—sitting next to shelves full of hot sauces with names like Whoop-Ass.

We walked along Oceanside Beach and Manzanita Beach. Shoes off, looking for agates. I didn't know what an agate looked like, but the beaches in this area are some of the best spots in the world to find them. We studded our pockets with maybe-agates that were also maybe-glass and maybe-rocks. We visited Munson Creek Falls, which jets down a 319-foot basalt cliff. And the Octopus Tree, an ancient Sitka spruce like an enormous candelabrum on the forest floor. Tradition has it that Native Americans shaped it as a burial tree to hold the canoes that cradled their departed.

At night we'd sit out on the balcony to watch romantic Oregon Coast sunsets, but all we'd get were skies full of cloud, dense and gray, like wet newspaper.

On my birthday we got dressed up and had dinner at a fancy restaurant right at the edge of Nehalem Bay. Dessert was flourless chocolate cake with crème anglaise and a cookie sticking out the top. And a candle. As I took a first fingertip taste of cream, a man ran through the restaurant door.

"Tsunami warning—everyone to higher ground!"

The owner of the place was at our table right away. She gave us her card and told us get going. We were up and out the door without paying, without dessert. Except that I did grab the cookie.

Highway 101 took us north. No idea where we were going, just stuck in the middle of the exodus. Ocean to our left and cliff face to our right, nothing but buzz on the radio, we followed a slow line of cars through dusk.

The cell phone: my mother. "Where are you, I've been watching TV and—"

"OK, so what's going on?"

Earthquake off the coast of Eureka. Tsunami warning from Mexico all the way to Alaska. We inched toward higher ground. Still hemmed in by cliff and ocean, we were a single lane of creeping wheels and brake lights. The map didn't show any roads leading away from the waterfront. I lost Mom, and then my sister was on the phone. With her two children to sing me Happy Birthday.

Stephen and I were perfect little lemmings. When everyone else stopped, we stopped. We were at a lookout, high above Manzanita Beach. We got out of the car. People stood at the short, thick stone wall overlooking the sea, like waiting for the show to start. Stephen said we were high enough, but I kept thinking about those newscasts of the Indian Ocean tsunami only six months before, all those people just swept away.

Down on the beach, sirens cried. Some voice over a loudspeaker was too far away to make out. A car up the road must have had its stereo on, because a tumble of drums ran over the sirens. A beating that grew louder as Stephen and I walked up the road, past the crowds. Step around the bend, and a group of men, five or six or more, hammered with mallets and whirled palms against all sorts of big, tribal-looking drums. It folded into one massive rhythm that rocked against the cliff face and out over the water, like Oregon pounding a prayer to the sea.

We took just a few more steps. A line of trees along the road opened in a V, and out over that sea glowed a billowy blaze of perfect Oregon sunset.

Stephen stood behind me, arms around my waist. And I was happy on the edge of the world, waiting for whatever was to come.

I didn't get a tsunami for my birthday, but the next day I got Bayocean.

The idea back in 1906 was that Bayocean, developed on a sand spit with the Pacific on one side and Tillamook Bay on the other, would become the Atlantic City of the West. They built hotels, a bowling alley, tennis courts, an open-air dancing pavilion, and a natatorium (I didn't know what that meant either) – a huge building that housed a movie theater and an immense heated pool complete with salt water and a wave machine. Because tourists love to travel all the way to the ocean to swim in a pool.

Bayocean was called the Playground of the Pacific Northwest, and by the 1920s, it was sinking into the sea.

The natatorium was unusable by 1932, completely gone by 1939. By 1954, the spit washed out and turned Bayocean into a soggy, dilapidated island, and in 1960, the last house fell into the Pacific.

Now, between the work of a new jetty and Mother Nature, it was a spit again, and Stephen and I stepped along sandy dirt, wildflowers, and snarls of blackberry. I pointed to a spiraling of two black birds high up there and said, "Turkey vultures."

"That's unpleasant," Stephen said. "Let's call them

Oregon condors."

I'd pictured us walking along a sandy mud shore, looking for old pieces of buried foundation, but the trail now took us into a forest, which swallowed us up like the sea swallowed up Bayocean.

Gawky, young spruce trees grew up over our heads and spread out as far as we could see. The winding trail started to lose itself in the tall grasses and yellow scotch broom. Then the trees gave way to a stretch of sand dunes and waist-high reeds. It dipped down, then rose to a crest. Nothing but reeds waving against sky.

As we topped the hill, the world opened up.

Stephen half-whispered: "Oh..."

You discover something and it belongs to you. No matter that others have discovered it, too. Bayocean. A sudden wide, beautiful beach. Clean ivory sand sloped down to the thundering, sun-dazzled blue.

And we had it all to ourselves.

We kept thinking, as we walked along the shore, that we'd see somebody else. The salt breeze was soft and the sun warm. From the water, the beach ran up to a long stretch of cliff capped with scrubby brush and exposed tree roots, like the earth here had just dropped out from under itself.

Which, frankly, can happen with anything. Whether you're Lewis and Clark finding paradise (and then hating all the rain) or a perpetual tourist, leaving her career for an ice cream scoop and true love, based on the sturdy foundation of a stream of e-mails and the paintings of a man in a dress.

I sat, then lay back. Spread my arms and legs in arcs. Sand angel. My jeans and shirt filled with Oregon grit. Stephen said, "Now you'll just have to take your clothes off."

"I will if you will," I said.

For a moment he just looked at me.

Then he dragged his shirt over his head.

Lewis and Clark never got naked on their frontier (or maybe they did; there's some speculation about Mr. Meriwether), but if they didn't, they sure should have. There is no more lovely-crazy-free feeling in the world. Bayocean stretched out, a forever of sand and sea, and I removed every thread of my old life. The jeans I'd bought in Memphis, the top from Buffalo, the socks, shoes, underwear I'd picked up who knows where. Now all I felt was Oregon sand on my back, Oregon air on my face. All of me touching this place I loved. This place and this man.

•

The breeze was starting to chill. The sea swished and sucked back more sand. Maybe we'd turn around, walk back down the shore, and find that Bayocean had come alive and swallowed up our neat pile of clothes. I wanted to walk forever. Feel this free forever. Then my eyes out across the water found the white shimmer of a boat. Not close. But close enough.

Up ahead, a goldfinch swept down onto a twist of exposed root.

"Kiss me at the yellow bird," I said, "and we'll head back."

• • •

Gigi Little now works as In-Store Merchandising and Promotions Coordinator for Powell's City of Books. Her short story "Shanghaied" was published in the book *Portland Noir*, and during her circus days, she wrote and illustrated two children's picture books: *Wright Vs. Wrong* and *The Magical Trunk*. She and her husband, Stephen, live in Northwest Portland.

3,000 Miles WNW

COLIN REA

Eight years ago, when I moved from southwest Virginia to central Oregon, I left behind the lush, verdant forests of Barbara Kingsolver's *Prodigal Summer* and entered the clear-cut hills of Ken Kesey's *Sometimes a Great Notion.* I became an Oregonian (which I much prefer to the term, Oregander). I already possessed the requisite love of microbrewed beer and the correct politics, more blue than red, when I settled into my new region, new state, new home. What I found was a place and people teeming with pride and awash in contradiction. But don't despair, fellow Oregonians—I offer that observation as high praise.

In 1971, then-Governor Tom McCall famously told CBS News: "Come visit us again and again. This is a state of excitement. But for heaven's sake, don't come here to live." Conventional wisdom says Oregonians fancy themselves as New Englanders do. They take pride in the roots they put down and slap OREGON NATIVE bumper stickers on their Subarus and hybrid Hondas. (Yes, the greening of America has pushed aside the Volkswagen in favor of trendy Japanese bubble cars; never mind that the new diesel VW gets better mileage.) And yet, seemingly everyone in the state moved here from somewhere else, especially from the somewhere else known as the Upper Midwest. Badgers, Gophers, Buckeyes, and Wolverines are all well represented in the Willamette (rhymes with dammit) Valley and beyond, mixing with the resident Ducks and Beavers. Travel to southern Oregon and you'll meet Californians who cashed out three-bedroom houses in order to buy bigger homes for half the price near our beloved Shakespeare Festival. Up north, Portland attracts the young hipsters from colleges across the country who know that Seattle went south when Cobain blew the lid off the grunge movement.

Yes, we Oregonians want you to come for a drink and a story, but then kindly head home and tell a friend.

With 12 percent unemployment, we need the tourism dollars. Dig a little deeper though, and remove the short memory of Americans that make a hundred and fifty years seem like an epoch, and you'll find that this state has few citizens living outside the reservations that can claim anything close to native status. While participating in a statewide read as part of Oregon's sesquicentennial celebration, University of Oregon journalism professor and author Lauren Kessler demonstrated this each time she asked for a show of hands during readings. Three hundred hands became thiry, then three, and then none as these literary Oregonians were asked who was born in Oregon, and then whose parents, and whose grandparents and great-grandparents were born here.

Happily, an Oregonian becomes so with a driver's license (good for eight years; make that picture count) and the baptism of the first fall rain. And what of that rain? I have now worn out my first license and seen the sun go on sabbatical each October. I grew up outside of Washington, D.C., a child of the summer who lived at the pool and became a lifeguard the minute I was old enough to do so. My childhood was blessed with four perfectly balanced seasons.

Not so in the Pacific Northwest. I was worried how my body and mind would react to seven months of rain and five of sun. Would I end up as Jack Torrance in *The Shining* (which, by the way, was filmed in Oregon at the Timberline Lodge on Mount Hood)? Would I require massive doses of Vitamin D to survive the monsoon? Nope. The secret of the wet Northwest? It rarely rains in Oregon. Rather, it mists. There is always water in the air, but good luck trying to figure out where it comes from. Up, down, sideways? No, it really just hangs there. I actually find this a delightful way to go through fall and winter. Then, just when it seems to be too much, the sun comes out and stays. Months of hiking, camping, climbing, biking, canoeing, and canoodling in the outdoors tires us out until we anticipate the first cloudy day, the first hint of our mist. Sure, we'll grumble outwardly about the humidity, but inside we're delighted. We get to light a fire, settle back into a comfortable chair, and read.

And we read a lot. Perhaps it is borne of our hippie legacy, but Oregonians (and our kith and kin up north in Washington) are a literary bunch. I've worked in bookstores and libraries for most of my life, in two very different parts of the country, and if a book is on the *New York Times* Bestseller List, we helped put it there. Think *Snow Falling on Cedars* and *The Art of Racing in the Rain.* Not only do we read, but we write. Visit your local independent bookstore and plant yourself in the Sci-Fi/Fantasy section. Start reading author bios and notice now many of them "Live somewhere in Oregon" or "Live on the Oregon Coast." You can't swing your dreadlocks in my state without hitting a Hugo Award winner. We also boast literary legends both dead (Ken Kesey) and alive (Barry Lopez) and a hero to all preteens (Beverly Cleary).

Life is not all pretty and perfect in Oregon. A state that grew up on a steady diet of lumber mills and commercial fishing is living in a present that knows a blown housing bubble and depleted waters. Our schools need more money, and many Oregonians have no library service. As a state, we're upside down on our mortgage. We have too much meth, too few jobs, and a reputation for putting spotted owls and spawning fish ahead of the working man. But we have the one thing that will always transcend these issues: a strength and diversity of people. Cattlemen in the high desert, aging hippies in Eugene—farmers outside Corvallis, business-minded folk in Portland; these are all Oregonians, and they keep this state balanced and their differences engender the need for cooperation, which makes living here a fine thing.

Eight years in the Beaver State and I feel right at home. When I travel east, I find the trees disturbingly round, not pointy, and I wonder why there aren't drive-up coffee stands on every corner. I'm no Oregon expert yet; in fact, I had to double-check to be sure I had the state nickname correct. There are still mysteries to uncover. Why, for instance, does *everyone* in Oregon either own or covet an RV that costs more than their home? Why do the grass seed farmers torch their fields each year, dotting the horizon with mushroom clouds? And ceiling heat? Don't get me started on that one.

Eventually I'll know the answers to these and other important questions. Until then, I'll enjoy raising my own Oregonians on a steady diet of damp, nourishing literature.

• • •

Colin Rea is the director of the Fern Ridge Library District in Veneta, Oregon. A former bookseller and PNBA board member, he may be the only Oregonian to dislike the Grateful Dead. His favorite foods are scotch and sandwiches.

Honeychild

APRIL NABHOLZ

I arrived in Oregon in the back seat of a crew cab pickup truck with a horse trailer and my mule in tow. I had known the woman in the front seat for only a few weeks, but she'd offered to haul my mule, Honeychild, and me from Spokane, Washington, to Enterprise, Oregon.

Honeychild and I were hitchhiking, in a sense, from the Bob Marshall Wilderness in western Montana to Corvallis, Oregon, just forty miles inland of the Pacific Ocean, which neither of us had ever seen. I was from Pennsylvania and my mule was from Wyoming. How we came to be stranded in the Bob Marshall Wilderness is another story, probably more sensational than this one, but that is a story for later and this is the story for now—the story of how I came to Oregon—rain-drenched Oregon, lush Oregon, dry Oregon: the place that caught and kept me.

My first sight of Oregon came as a shock. All summer long, as I crept my way across sun-parched Montana, I'd been dreaming about the lush rewards awaiting me in the Pacific Northwest. I'd heard tales of monster trees, veils of lichens, treasure troves of mushrooms, and bright green rolling hills of vibrant, verdant, super-sized forest. My summer on the Great Plains had left my throat dry and my soul thirsty. My Appalachian roots were threatening to wither up and die. I needed a fix of woodland and rain. In Oregon, I was sure I would find respite.

When my mule and I are dropped off at the Enterprise Fairgrounds, square in the northeast corner of the state, I believe there must be some mistake. We aren't in a temperate rainforest at all; we are in the middle of a desert. I pull myself to the top rail of a fence and stare forlornly westward.

I had been led to believe the state was lush, hilly, and green, but what I see is a thirsty, scrubby expanse of barely anything. The ground is hard and dusty, and I see scarcely a tree. As a matter of survival, I swallow my disappointment and carry hay and water to my mule.

To the north I can see snow-peaked mountains—the Eagle Caps, I am told—and hear that nearby is a legendary gorge that runs deeper than the Grand Canyon itself. Hell's Canyon, they call it, and it is wilder, rougher, crueler, and more beautiful, plunging more than a mile deep into the earth from Oregon's eastern rim. I lay awake my first night in Oregon shivering in my sleeping bag under a starving moon and starry sky.

From Enterprise I catch a ride west as far as Corvallis, where I find a setting more closely resembling my exaggeratedly verdant preconceptions of the state. Oregon, I discover, is divided into two distinct climates by the Cascade Mountain Range, which runs north to south through the state. East of the Cascades is Oregon's dry side, where rainfall is scarce year-round; west of the range is the lush side of Oregon, where rainfall is heavy and constant through the winter season and virtually nonexistent during summer.

Nestled ten miles west of the I-5 corridor, safely on the lush side of the state, Corvallis sits in the heart of the Willamette Valley between the Coast Range and the Cascades. Months later, driving south through the valley toward Eugene, a native Oregonian will proudly describe to me the arrival of Oregon Trail pioneers in the valley and how it seemed to them that they had chanced upon paradise, how they settled down here, and never budged again. They were sheep farmers, he says, and even now, some of their great-grandchildren's great-grandchildren are grazing sheep in the valley.

My mule, Honeychild, is a hefty draft cross weighing 1,500 pounds. She is the largest mule I've ever seen, and she's fresh off the Montana range and half wild. I find a stable on the edge of town where I can work in exchange for board. At night I sleep at the edge of her paddock beneath a gnarled white oak. When she is lonely during the night, she reaches up to shake the dry, rattling branches, waking me in a rain of acorns and dead leaves. "Hush, Chi," I soothe. "Go back to sleep." She sighs and fidgets, unused to the sounds and smells. One night she pulls my shoes into her paddock while I am sleeping, and another night she drags away my tarp.

I've arrived at the end of the dry season, and the rains are expected to begin within weeks. Meanwhile the dust rolls across the valley in a haze each morning, and I wake with dust caking my sleeping bag and hair. I roll over to watch the early light strike against the wall of the Coast Range from the east, and see dust devils swirling across the valley. I am desperate for rain, crazy for moisture. Each day, the sky maintains perfect, unthreatened blue.

Standing under the oak one day, a fellow in a cowboy hat comes over to name the mountains for me. He points across the valley to the lumpy green range, where one big mountain hulks above the rest.

"That's Mary's Peak," he says with pride. "The tallest girl in the whole range. She holds snow year-round, but most people don't know that. From the valley floor she looks melted by about June." He pauses in his monologue. "Or July, if spring is late. Don't plant your tomatoes til the snow is gone from Mary's Peak, that's what the old people say." He walks away, horse in tow.

Mary's Peak looks green and forested, but the valley dividing us is hung with dust and smoke. September, I learn, is the end of grass seed season, when the seed growers set flame to their dry fields to refertilize them, and I am standing in a valley known as the grass seed capital of the world. Oregon is the world's largest producer of cool-season forage seed, and grass seed is one of the state's primary agricultural crops. The Willamette Valley is home to 480,000 of Oregon's 530,000 seed-producing acres.

The controversy surrounding field burning has been long and loud. A temporary moratorium on field burning was enforced in 1988 after a cloud of smoke blew across I-5 just south of Portland, obscuring the highway during high rush traffic. In the mayhem that ensued, twenty-three vehicles were crumpled against each other and seven people were left dead, another thirty-eight wounded. Since then, increasingly strict regulations have reduced the number of burned fields to about 10 percent of the valley's seed-producing acreage, though debate and controversy persists.

My new home, I discover, is full of food. A Gravenstein apple tree stands just outside the bunkhouse door, and a grove of Golden Delicious gather at the end of the lane. The apple harvest is heavy this fall, and unburdening the trees' painfully bowed limbs feels near to an act of grace. I find a huge bag of Krusteaz pancake mix on the top shelf of a kitchen cupboard. Pancakes become the basis of my breakfasts, lunches, and dinners, covered variably with apples or blackberries.

Blackberries. The blackberries are a discovery unto themselves. Vast hedges of them line every fence and field edge. The berries are beyond anything I've ever imagined. I never believed all of those poems about blackberries before; at home in Pennsylvania, we didn't eat the tart little fruits. Here in Oregon, I finally understand what the poets are raving about. The biggest berries are as large as the biggest digit on my thumb, and sweeter, richer, and more flavorful than any berry I've ever tasted.

Within several weeks of my arrival, I find a job in a little independent bookstore downtown. My résumé, drawn up on the spot, consists of several handwritten pages decorated with sketches of my mule. The bookstore is one of the oldest in Oregon, and has occupied the same downtown address for nearly four decades. A lifelong book devotee, I am happy for the work and glad for the chance to meet so many Oregonians face-to-face. I find a room to rent a few blocks away from the bookstore, and my daily landscape is established.

For $295 each month, I am granted a dingy room

encroached on both sides by the eaves of the tiny house it apexes. The plaster on the walls is cracked and discolored, but there is one south-facing window, happily blinded by the upper branches of a magnolia growing below. After a season of life on the trail, I feel I have fallen into the lap of luxury. Four other people share the house, crammed together in the other rooms and basement. Each morning we visit the one bathroom in sequence, each taking no more time than necessary to perform the morning's duties.

Though I have a job, I won't have a paycheck for four weeks, and the kitchen shelf I've been issued is tidy and nearly empty. I long for the familiar apple trees and blackberry hedges lining my mule's paddock five miles distant. Hunger fuels my first explorations of my new neighborhood.

Just as at the stable, I find food everywhere. Plums dangle over the sidewalk and roll into the street on the corner of 13th and D, just several houses up from an empty lot housing a pear tree, several grapevines, and an apple tree. I find figs in half a dozen public places, as well as quince and even blueberries. Yard after yard reveals sturdy vegetable plants tidily tucked in among the flowerbeds. Neighbors suffering from overabundance give me tomatoes, squash, chard, and even fresh chicken eggs. In the alley behind a bakery, I find a plastic trash bin reliably full of day-old loaves several days each week. I buy myself a jar of peanut butter and am in want of nothing.

Before settling into a regular work schedule, I take a weekend trip to the Steens Mountains in southeastern Oregon with my new housemates. I am appalled at the vastness of their flat surroundings; the gazillion individual hues of white, gray, pink, yellow, and green that haunt the sunrise over the salt flats; and the heat of the hot springs gurgling up from mud in the earth. I am astonished beyond belief at the sharpness of the mountain peaks, the freshness of their crags, the perfection of their U-shaped glacial troughs. This range contains some of the best examples of glacial furrows in the world. I stand on the edge of a cliff with my toes tingling from the height, my fingers numb from icy wind. I stand transfixed not from cold but from the sudden minuteness of my size now held against the enormity of the world. I had forgotten, perhaps, my smallness in the grander scheme of things, forgotten that the world revolved around something larger than myself.

We camp one night beside a lake, another in a rocky field where I see a rattlesnake slither away. Sagebrush flavors the air with its astringent scent and its yellow blossoms wake the gray-blue morning before sunrise. Our third campsite is in the shelter of yellow aspens. We wake to rain in the night, and in the morning our tents are glazed with ice. On our way home we stop for a hike in the Cascades, where rain graces the earth in every season. I see huge trees, thick green moss, enormous ferns, glassy black shards of obsidian, and, in the distance, the white peaks of volcanoes. I wonder if my roots could really grow here—if this is one of the rare places on earth that could ever sever me from my eastern home ground, which I had believed without doubt, until now, I was forever inseparable from.

The rains set in during my seventh week in Oregon. I am initially relieved; I've been thirsty for months. The ground soaks up the water like a sponge, and in the mild temperatures a sort of second spring erupts. The grass turns green and lush again, seedlings sprout in the garden, here and there a flower blooms. But the sun has sunk low by this point, and the light is dim even at midday. Even warm soil and rain can't make up for a lack of sunlight, and the half-grown seedlings remain stuck in immaturity.

My early joy for the rain fades after several weeks of monotonous drizzle. I am used to the crashing thunder and lightning of the east, the thrashing deciduous foliage, the quick returns to brilliant blue sky and crisp fall air. At home, the thunderstorms come like manic temper tantrums and are over just as quickly as they came; here, the weeping eternal drizzle feels like long-term depression. Incredulously, I watch native Oregonians rejoicing in the dreary weather. "Old Mossy Backs," a man named Farmer Frank calls them, for they are Pacific Northwestern to the core. I hear my coworkers wax enthusiastic over the fog and the mist, the long dark nights, and the unbeatable mushroom harvest.

I embrace the rain as best I can. I crawl on my belly through decomposing leaves and dripping underbrush in the dark forests, filling soggy paper bags with firm golden chanterelles and brown boletes. I wear my tall rubber boots to the farm to visit Honeychild, and I borrow a suit of rain gear so I can bicycle through the wet weather in comfort. My attempts are wholehearted but, in the end, mostly futile.

On Christmas Eve I lie wrapped in wool blankets on top of hay bales in Honeychild's stall while cold rain drizzles down the roof of the barn and blows in through cracks in the walls. I wait for her to speak to me at midnight, but instead she tries to pull the hay bales out from underneath me. I cover my ears to plug out the noise of the rain and remember instead the white Vermont blizzards that enveloped me last winter and the dazzling blindness of the ensuing daylight. I will try to love the rain again tomorrow, but for tonight, I let myself wish I were home.

Spring brings the joy of sunshine again, and with it a lushness beyond my prior concepts. I visit the coast, the mountains, the waterfalls. I find a job with a field crew, I plant a garden, I spy on elk, I ride Honeychild, I bicycle, I buy a pressure canner, and I believe I might never leave Oregon. I fall in love, I break my heart, and I fall in love again. I visit the east coast and return to Corvallis happily but with new apprehension, for I remember now how much I love the east: the fireflies, the thunderheads, the sassafras trees.

•

After a year in Oregon, I've begun to feel like a local. I walk the same route to work each day, and pass the same people at the same intersections. I greet customers by name all day long in the bookstore, and they greet me by mine, inquire after my mule, and offer invitations to dinner, to housesit, to potlucks or morning coffee. My garden gave me a solid harvest this summer, and fifty quarts of tomatoes sit beaming on my kitchen shelves among pickled beans, applesauce, peaches, and pickles. Honeychild grazes contentedly down the road. I have a car with Oregon license plates.

Will I stay? I have plans to winter elsewhere this year, outside of our country, so I can see it whole and from a distance again. From that vantage point, I think, I'll be able to feel which coast tempts me most. What will draw me back? The mammoth sacred trees in Northern California? The small towns scattered across New England? The contentment Oregonians exude in rainfall? The rolling farmland and peach orchards surrounding my home in Pennsylvania? The fireflies, the lightning, and deciduous forests? The rocky Oregon coast, the wilderness, the sagebrush desert, the blackberries?

I feel my roots testing the soil, my branches testing the air.

• • •

April Nabholz grew up in rural Pennsylvania, attended Warren Wilson College in Asheville, North Carolina, and worked as a dishwasher in Montpelier, Vermont. After traveling in Asia post-graduation, she vowed not to leave the country again until she had seen the western half of her own homeland. She traveled to Oregon in 2008 and settled in Corvallis, Oregon, where she plays daily at Grass Roots Books and Music.

The Colors of Oregon

KIMBERLY SEITS

Daily life sometimes gets in the way of reflecting on the beauty of my state, but when I'm having a really bad day, all I have to do is take a short drive and I am instantly reminded of why I love living here.

In the summer I enjoy traveling west towards the coast. There I am greeted, after long winding roads under an endless canopy of green, by the tawny sand and majestic blue of the Pacific Ocean—unless it's a stormy day. On such days I'm bombarded by countless varieties of whites, grays, blacks, greens, and purples, which all intertwine to tell me a story of anger. Although such shows are usually reserved for winter, summer storms do occasionally burst forth upon the coast.

Every now and then, as I travel through the coastal mountain range, I don't make it all the way to the beach, deciding instead to stop and listen to the musical serenade of any one of the numerous creeks and rivers that bubble near the road. On such days I sit quietly and watch as the sunlight peeks through and lights up the plants around me as if it were an artist experimenting with every shade of green. Occasionally a bright red, yellow, or black will pop out of the scene as berries and flowers attempt to lure animals.

Too soon the days of summer begin to shorten and we know that winter is on its way. Oregon does not always bless the eyes with a true fall season; sometimes the rain pushes us right into winter. However, when nature does decide to grant us a fall show, it is nothing less than spectacular. One cannot go more than a few blocks (even in the densest city areas) without seeing a tree or two in its fall coat. Yet that does not even hint at the glory one can see by taking a trip through the rolling landscape of the Willamette Valley when entire hills turn to fire. The golds, oranges, reds, purples, yellows and browns all dance as the wind rustles down the valley.

As fall fades, Oregonians begin to experience the drab days of pre-winter. The clouds seem to wrap us up like a giant down comforter. But even through these cold wet days, if one looks hard enough, color can be found. Yellow blurs whiz in and out of traffic as bicyclists don bright slickers. Young children walk to school with bright umbrellas. Nature even teases us with rainbows once in a while.

When your spirits are overwhelmed with the grayness, a short drive east begins to lift them. Heading up to Mount Hood one is quickly surrounded by evergreen trees that bring back a sense of life and hope, evoking thoughts of Christmas and joy. Beyond the snow-lined passes of the Cascade Range, an invisible line comes into view. Suddenly there are no more Douglas firs, and as the eye scans the horizon, it is filled with Ponderosa pines and the red clay soils that signal the desert. Black cliffs and rock formations provide a backdrop that sharply contrasts with the thinly wooded forests along the roadside. In Sisters or Bend, the sunsets and sunrises are amazing to behold, as the sun gleams just under the edge of the clouds in every hue between pink and blue.

Finally, winter storms begin and ice pelts our homes and cars, making everything gleam and glisten under a clear coat of frost. As for the color white, finding more than a handful of days when snow blanketed the ground. Recently however, this seems to be changing. The white flakes seem to be falling and sticking more and more. I notice this trend because of school closures. Growing up, I could count on one hand the total number of days I ever missed from school due to snow—meaning that two inches fell overnight. But now snow days seem to happen at least once a year.

In fact, last year the entire Portland metro area shut down for almost two weeks and the snow on the ground actually came up to my knees. Seeing everything everything covered in white was an amazing sight, the cars shapeless blobs lining the street. Little brown birds flocked to the crabapple tree in my yard with its bright red berries, the only visible fruit in the area. It was such a joy and wonder to wake up every day for a week to the blindingly bright crispness of snow all around the house.

Eventually the rain washes away all the ice and snow, and things become drab again, but usually not for long. The lengthening days bring the smells and thoughts of spring. Green shoots start flaring up everywhere, and every house has at least one flowerbed in its yard.

The colors of spring surround us with yellows,

whites, and oranges as daffodils blanket the roadsides. Soon, more and more flowers pop up, and towns drape hanging flower baskets from light poles, while garden centers tempt us to take home more plants than we have room for. As if all that color wasn't enough, we have farms that specialize in growing and selling the springtime blooms. Swan Island Dahlia is one of the area's most famous farms; wandering through the rows and rows of color is an amazing trip.

As spring hits its peak, we find every small town has a local farmers market open on weekends to sell, share ,and celebrate the bounty of our valley. The white tents shade us as the dog days of summer approach and we continue to celebrate and root through the marvelous fruits, vegetables, and nuts that provide a feast for the eyes as well as stomachs. As summer days lengthen, I again find myself heading out to the coast to start my year of colors all over again.

• • •

Kimberly Seits has a Master's degree in Library Science and currently works on call as a reference librarian for three different libraries, two in Clackamas County and one in Washington County. She has lived in Oregon for more than thirty years and sees no reason to ever leave the state.

Land of Oz

KAREN MUNRO

We moved back to Oregon on a day that was both sunny and rainy. It was sunny in California, which we were leaving; it was raining in Oregon, which was home. As my wife and I drove the rental van north on I-5 through the Siskiyou Mountains, we crossed an invisible line in the land. Almost without warning, we passed from sunshine into a summer squall. Rain beat down from a low, pewter sky and hit the pavement so hard it bounced right back up in a mist. The windshield became an Impressionist painting, the trailing smears of taillights framed by looming black trees. The wipers churned and squeaked.

I'd been looking forward to seeing the sign that I knew must be there on the side of the road, somewhere around Siskiyou Summit: Welcome to Oregon. But I was too busy trying to find the road through the downpour to see the sign when we passed it, and I had to guess at the point when we crossed the border. The storm was as good as any sign that I was home again.

On the Oregon side of the mountains, after a hair-raising descent through Tolkienian clouds into the green valley below, we pulled up to a gas station, where my wife used a cement pylon to scrape a fine layer of paint off the side of the moving van. We got out to admire the damage, and noticed something we hadn't seen before. There was a hole in the van's roof. In dry, balmy California, this hadn't mattered. Here in Oregon, it was something to consider.

"Did you catch what was on the radio just now?" my wife asked me, as we stood trying to remember what was packed in the top right corner of the van. "Goodbye Yellow Brick Road."

California was behind us; ahead lay a gray twilight, a cold mist, and after another rainy half-day's drive, the strangely thrilling iron-and-concrete bridges of Portland, where we were going to try to live.

We'd moved from Eugene, Oregon, to California a couple of years before for a brief dalliance with the Bay Area. Now we were coming back—circling homeward, I felt, although neither of us is from Oregon. I was born in Canada, my wife in Baton Rouge. Still, crossing the border between sunny California and rainy Oregon felt momentous and complicated in the same ways that every trip back to Canada has always felt to me. I felt nostalgic, excited, eager to notice the smallest changes in the landscape, amazed at all I'd managed to forget.

How did Oregon come to have this hold on me? It's hard to say. I'm Canadian—you can hear it when I talk, when I say "sorry" with a long, hollow O, the humble shibboleth that betrays every secret Canadian. In the most basic ways, I'm an outsider in this country. The formal term is "resident alien," and in this case, the term is apt. Alienation is built into my life in this country—not just because I'm here on the sufferance of a limited-term work permit, but also because while I'm here, the best and biggest part of my domestic life is invalid. My wife is a woman, and so am I. From an American point of view we aren't married, and we have no household. Period.

The message from my semi-adopted country is cheerless, clear, and to-the-point: You aren't at home here, no matter how long you hang around. Don't take your shoes off, don't sit down. Don't get comfortable.

Even shorter, even pointier: Go home.

There are plenty of good reasons why Oregon isn't everyone's Emerald City. Forget metaphor, forget fancy talk about civil liberties and "belonging." Start with climate. Move to Oregon—at least the western half of the state, where most people live—and you'd better like rain. Most years, the winter rains start in October and last until May. They're not mild or sultry, either; the cold has a wet, leaden, inescapable quality. It gets into your bones. In summer, the average temperature of the ocean along the north-central coast is a lively fifty-five degrees. Boating guides offer helpful tables to show how smartly the water will freeze you to death.

Then take politics. Oregon likes them mysterious and volatile. The ballot measure—essentially a petition-driven demand for new law—has a long history in Oregon, and since practically anyone can propose a measure, practically everyone does. The state legislature meets only every two years, which means things have to get done fast, by legislators who hold day jobs as well as their government posts. Every budget year offers the citizenry of Oregon a kind of dire political theater—a long period of uncertainty followed by a series of late-breaking pronouncements, a scramble of reaction, and sometimes the invocation of the "kicker," the regulation requiring the state to return any year's excess tax revenue directly to the taxpayers. Not surprisingly, the kicker has made it hard for Oregon to build up much of a rainy-day fund, so to speak.

If you still think Oregon's for you, consider carefully what you'll do when you get there. Oregon's economy has traditionally been based on primary industry and farming: forestry, fisheries, ranching, and niche products such as hazelnuts, pears, and Christmas trees. In the past few decades, the state has started to branch out into the utopian and forward-looking: solar power, wind power, semiconductors. And in its inimitably quirky fashion, Oregon has plenty of jobs for gas jockeys—drivers are prohibited by law from pumping their own gas. But despite all this, at the time of this writing, Oregon is caught up in the fist of the same recession that is squeezing the country and the world, and the state is more than eleven percent unemployed.

Stand in a certain spot and view things just so, and Oregon is a cold, rainy hinterland perpetually teetering on the brink of bankruptcy. It's a crazy place to settle down, especially if you're not from here to start with. Especially if the odds are stacked against you, if the roadside sign isn't visible and the official welcome mat's been yanked inside. But things look different depending on who you are, and where you're coming from. They look different depending on where you happen to be standing.

My wife and I stood under the gas station canopy, out of the rain, while the attendant filled our tank. We studied the scrape along the side of the moving van and considered opening up the back to check on the state of the boxes inside. That, we decided, was a bad idea: contents may shift during transport.

We were due that night in a cheap hotel in Ashland, just into Oregon. The next morning we'd start the second leg of the trip, continuing north up I-5, the hemline freeway that stitches up the west coast of the country from Mexico to Canada. On the way we'd pass by Eugene, the sweet, dippy little college town where I once worked as a librarian for the University of Oregon, and where I still store a fraction of my heart. The land beside the freeway would be green and lush, acre after acre of pastures for sheep and horses. Hawks and falcons would perch on the fence posts, and turkey vultures would circle the buttes.

We'd reach Portland early in the gray afternoon. As we followed the freeway toward the Willamette River crossing, we'd pass beneath the gleaming silver capsule of the passenger gondola on its way up to Oregon Health Sciences University. It's good luck to see the gondola cross above you, a little blessing from the city gods. For a minute or two after that, we'd ride the fine, unforgiving line of the I-5 bridge, hundreds of feet over the wide cold river. Ahead of us, half-hidden in clouds, massive and austere, great and terrible: Mount Hood.

Going home is a problem for people like me who have adopted, or been adopted by, awkward or unlikely places. Home, strictly speaking, must be Canada. It's where I was born, where I have citizenship, where I have full human rights. Oregon offers me a bare second-best: the right to work for a while, the lukewarm legal handshake of domestic partnership.

For people like me, Oregon, like Oz, seems like a place to wander for a while. A fascinating, frustrating place, a place that offers fields of poppies and cities made of emerald but nowhere to put down roots. Elton John had it right: you can follow the yellow brick road in search of a heart, a head, or whatever it is you're looking for—but sooner or later, you're going to have to click your heels together and come back to the real world. You're going to have to make your peace with imperfection and decide whether you can live with things as they are.

We didn't have to stop in Oregon. I-5 is the only freeway in the country that touches both Mexico and Canada. We could have kept following the dotted yellow line, the yellow brick road, all the way up through Washington to British Columbia, a place that would welcome us both.

We didn't keep going. We took our exit, followed our map, and found our new apartment just as a light rain began to fall. Next door to us, we quickly learned, was an apartment building run by a mental health agency. The tenants were sick people, poor people, people with problems; people who couldn't get along in the world without a helping hand.

It kept raining. We started the hard, fast business of moving in, hustling up and down the truck ramp, lugging soggy boxes in our weary arms. After a while a thin woman came out of the apartment next door and stood watching us. When we said hello, she smiled a wide, gap-toothed smile and said her name was Mary. I didn't think about it at the time, but it's likely that if she hadn't landed the agency apartment next door to us, Mary would have been homeless. Not metaphorically homeless, the way I sometimes feel, but actually homeless, the way lots of people are.

She disappeared, then came back a little while later and stood beside the ramp to hand us a sprig of flowers. They looked like the flowers you see in restaurant bud vases: a grape hyacinth, a rosebud. They were not in the prime of their lives. Mary said, Welcome to the neighborhood.

We found a glass somewhere and put the flowers in it. They sat on the windowsill for the next few days, blooming casually and brightly, as if they had their roots in solid earth.

• • •

Karen Munro is the head of the University of Oregon Portland Library and Learning Commons in Portland. She has an MFA in fiction from the Iowa Writers' Workshop and has published stories in *Grain*, *Glimmer Train*, and elsewhere.

Oregon Haikus

SHIRLEY THOMAS

SHORE ACRES STATE PARK

Gather and commune
Vast green edge of ocean roar
Touch in quiet space

CANNERY PIER, ASTORIA

Echo time gone by
Now bounty of connections
Proof our ship came in.

Shirley Thomas works at the Chemeketa Community College Library in Salem, Oregon.

WASHINGTON

STATE NICKNAME Evergreen State

STATE MOTTO Al-ki (Chinook word meaning "by and by")

STATE SONG "Washington, My Home"

STATE TREE Western hemlock

STATE FISH Steelhead trout

STATE FOSSIL Columbian mammoth

STATE GEM Petrified wood

STATE TRIVIA:

• Washington State produces more apples than any other state in the union.

• Everett is the site of the world's largest building, Boeing's final assembly plant.

• Washington is home to North America's largest land mollusk, a banana slug that grows up to 9 inches long.

• The percentage of non-religious people in Washington is the highest of any state, and church membership is among the lowest of all states.

- Washington State has more bookstores and coffee bean roasters per capita and its residents have more college degrees per capita than any other state.
- Washington produces 70 percent of the nation's hops used to brew beer. Possibly to combat beer breath, it also produces a majority of the nation's mint.
- Washington has the largest ferry system in the nation; 26 million passengers travel by ferry each year.
- The state of Washington is the only state to be named after a United States president. Before it became a state, the territory was called Columbia, after the Columbia River. When it was granted statehood, the name was changed to Washington, supposedly so people wouldn't confuse it with The District of Columbia.
- Famous Washingtonians: Jimi Hendrix, Sherman Alexie, Kurt Cobain, Bing Crosby, Thea Christiansen Foss, Bill Gates, Adam West, Christal Quintasket, Dale Chihuly, Frank Herbert, John Stockton, Gary Larson

Washington Ghost Story

REM RYALS

When I was a teenager, I worked at a summer camp near Leavenworth, a small mountain town near the geographical center of Washington State. There, on warm summer nights, with the sweet smell of ponderosa pines in the windy air and the distant roar of Icicle Creek in our ears, we heard the story of the Leavenworth Nurse.

She was a nurse who worked at the hospital nearby in the 1950s. Her husband was a logger, and his arm was severed in a horrible accident at the mill. He was rushed to the hospital, where he died on the operating table. In all the confusion, no one made the connection that the nurse was on duty, and she learned about what happened when she found his arm in the Emergency Room. Just lying there, the wedding ring still on its finger, the plaid shirt hanging off in tatters. They were newlyweds, deeply in love, and in the story, at that moment, she went completely, irrevocably insane. Her hair turned sheet white and she ran screaming out of the hospital into the nearby woods. She was never heard from again; well, at least not by anyone except small children, young teenagers, and a variety of other people unlucky enough to encounter her in the woods, where she murdered them with an ax. Also, the arm disappeared as well, leaving behind its own victim, an orderly with vicious strangulation marks around his neck. Over the coming years these two specters terrorized the surrounding countryside, killing many, leaving mysterious remains of campfires and gutted animals. Depending on who was telling the story, the nurse was a beautiful, silver-haired rescuer of lost children or a screaming, ax-wielding, bloodstained vision of female revenge.

For a long time I believed this story was true. I mean, I knew it wasn't true, but it seemed to express some essential truth about these mountains, something about beauty and danger.

•

Soon after this it was time for college, and I crossed those very same mountains and journeyed to Seattle, the misty, evergreen metropolis nicknamed "The Emerald City" by its residents. Roll your eyes if you will, but there is something in the dark trees, in the deep blue of the water and the sky—not to mention the mountain ranges on three horizons—that feels impossibly fertile and fantastic, especially to a boy coming from the arid eastern part of the state. I tried my best to follow the good Jesuits of Seattle University and work for the common good, but I was infected by a deep restlessness and a love of sensual experience. While all my friends were opting out for families and safe jobs—that's what I told myself—I wanted something more immediate, more real. The soundtrack in my mind at that time was the early romantic work of Jean Sibelius, a rollicking saga of danger, adventure, and discovery.

I felt fairly alone in this urge until I met Dorothy. On the surface she was just a business major from the suburbs, but I quickly learned she was a wild soul. Her idea of a good time was to go skydiving, or to head down to the highway and stick out her thumb, or take a cocktail of drugs and climb Mount Rainier. She had other boyfriends, none of whom knew of the others and at least one of whom thought he was her fiancé, but she didn't care. The first time we had sex it felt like a strange, cool resting place when I was finally inside her. The central feeling was not heat but space, and the center of it was in our heads. It was the first time I realized that sex could be about exploration, too. Our relationship peaked in a beautiful, sun-washed day hiking and bodysurfing along the Pacific coast, a day fueled by marijuana, amphetamines, and an epic hike along a cliffside trail. I've tried to describe this day many times in words, but it's lost to me now, although when I get around the roar of the ocean, I feel echoes of it still. Something about eternity, and the present moment as an edge, a wave, riding between birth and death. Foolishness, right?

At the time it didn't seem like foolishness but more like a movement I had to follow, as if it was stronger in certain places than others. I followed it right away from Dorothy, on to the Oregon Coast, then to San Francisco, and eventually to New York City, which seemed, at the time, the capital of all things New.

On the first night of my arrival there, after two

months incommunicado on the road, I received an urgent message to call a friend. I didn't get the friend but the friend's mother, who started stammering. Someone I knew had died, she said. It was Dorothy. She had hiked off-trail on a mountain in Palm Springs, California, and slipped on an ice field. A man she was with had managed to grab hold of a tree, but Dorothy had gone over the cliff. She had fallen almost a thousand feet.

I was overwhelmed with shock and sadness. And guilt. The breakup had not been pretty, and I wondered if I could have prevented her death had I been there. But even at the beginning I realized that this made some kind of weird sense, the way she had lived her life. It did not diminish my deep sense of wonder and loss, however. No matter how I tried, and try I would over the next five years, I would never have a single idea about what she had been thinking at the end, or how she had felt. I thought I had wanted mystery, and danger, but this . . . It was a mystery without a solution, a wall I just kept banging my head against.

In the meantime, New York was proving to be a dead end. It took me a few years to figure out why. What was missing? Oh yeah: trees, fresh air—nature. My plan now was to move to Mexico, but when I got back to Seattle, the salty wind blew off of Puget Sound like a drug, and the mist-enshrouded trees seemed to wrap around me like friendly arms. I was home.

I began to explore the mountains in earnest, pursuing again that sense of adventure, and probably Dorothy's spirit, too. The Glacier Peak Wilderness, Hurricane Ridge, the Enchantments, Stehekin—names as magical as the places they described. Hundreds of rarified cirques twinkling with wildflowers and glacial boulders and talking streams. I always emerged from these trips refreshed, filled with wonder, but one moment stands out. I was in the Bailey Range, deep in the Olympic Mountains, that almost ridiculously fairy-tale range on the edge of the continent. It was a foggy day in the high scree, freezing and eerily quiet, without even the high-pitched calls of the marmots for company. I was chilled to the bone and rushing to set up camp before dark and hypothermia set in. I turned around and there, where the fog had just been, was the giant mass of Mount Olympus. It was bathed in the florescent orange light of sunset and towering over me like some prehistoric monster. I literally dropped to my knees, overwhelmed for a split second by a wave of terror and awe. It only lasted a second, but in that second I knew a contradictory truth: that my time on this planet was less than a speck of dust, but that the author of all this grandeur had us well in hand.

Despite the strength of these experiences, I always had to go back to the lowlands, and it became obvious how never-ending this process was. Chasing God was hard work. Also, it began to seem a little dubious: what was I avoiding back in my "real life"? I didn't have far to look. My parents and grandparents had moved to the steppes of southeastern Washington in 1943. The reason: to build the Hanford Works, the reactor that produced the plutonium used in the bomb dropped on Nagasaki. This desert land had its own charm, of wind and sage and open sky—not to mention a little something called the Columbia River winding through it. But it was a lonely charm, at least for these new transplants from the East. For that reason, and the strange ethics of their work, and a hundred other reasons too numerous to recount here, most of them became alcoholics, at least in my family. And now here I was, holed up in a Seattle boardinghouse writing strange stories about people communicating with black cottonwood trees. Like my parents, my roots in this place were still tenuous.

But then I got lucky. I met Colleen.

She had brown hair, amber eyes, and a gentle manner. Despite a boisterous laugh, there was a deep stillness about her, like one of those apparently motionless hemlock trees in an old-growth forest, and I hardly noticed her the first few years I knew her. Then circumstances brought us closer together, and almost despite myself I found myself hanging around her, just wanting to sit next to her on the couch. But it wasn't sexual. That's what I told myself. And I believed it too, right up until the moment I kissed her. Then it was like an explosion, like being thrown somewhere far away, as though her stillness was necessary to cover a vast storm inside. When it was over, I felt disoriented, dizzy, blinking around at the foreign country to which I had returned.

We moved to Bellingham, a quiet town tucked away in the far northwest corner of the state, even darker and greener than Seattle, and what followed were many happy years. These consisted of listening to the fall gales roar through the tops of the Douglas firs outside, or swimming in the electric blue lakes in summer. Here's what I thought: I was done with all that dramatic stuff, driven by youth or drugs or God knows what. I had found my true love, and we would grow happily old together.

Colleen was not as flashy as Dorothy, as visibly restless, but she was just the same. She had already been to Africa for a year when we got together, and soon after she went back for six months. The earthiness of the life there appealed to her, and she recognized decades before most of us just what was at stake in our resource-consuming culture. Fervent about plastic recycling, pedestrian rights, and organic food, years before it was fashionable, she brought a quiet urgency to everything she did.

Her urgency probably came from her epilepsy. When I first knew her, her grand mal seizures were under control. But she picked up a parasite in Africa and her health steadily worsened. As the new century started, she enrolled in school to finish her anthropology degree, but her seizures continued unabated, resulting in an amazing list of injuries: broken ribs, tailbone, and wrist, and plastic surgery on a broken face. This was on top of panic attacks and hallucinations brought on by a wild mix of meds.

Still, for all this, I didn't see what was coming. I was visiting my parents in eastern Washington when I got a call from Colleen's mother in Tacoma, where Colleen was visiting. She'd had a seizure, her mom said, a really bad one. They had only just now got her breathing again. I was upset, certainly, but I had been through such seizures before. Or so I thought. I even went back to watching a movie with my parents.

It was the second phone call that did it. They were at the hospital, her mom said, and the doctor had told them that they would only know the extent of the damage if Colleen woke up. If she woke up? What the hell did that mean?

I suddenly knew what it meant, down to my toes. I had been through this before, after all. But this time I didn't have the luxury of watching from three thousand miles away. I was like that silly fellow who has his foot in the unwinding anchor rope and doesn't realize it until he's jerked off his feet and pulled over the side.

I drove over White Pass that night in a strange hallucinogenic fog—everything appeared puke orange. The next day I sobbed for hours at her bedside and begged her to come back. But there was no coming back, only a warm body and strange echoes of her spirit, and after four days in the ICU, we turned off the machines and let her go for good.

I was in for it now, the full-on grief experience, my own little journey into the underworld.

But something else happened: The morning after we took her off the machines, it dawned bright and sunny, the first such day since the ordeal had begun. I was driving down Pacific Avenue, toward her parents' house, and "the mountain was out," beautiful in front of me. Those who have lived in western Washington will know that I mean Mount Rainier, whose appearance is always stunning after weeks of gray; but this far south, which I had rarely been, the view is especially awe-inspiring. The mountain's 14,000-foot bulk rises quite unexpectedly from the sea-level plains below—there are no other mountains around it—and suddenly I was back in that place I had been with Mount Olympus years earlier. I knew, with the assurance of fact, that this was not the end for Colleen, but simply a transition. She had come to the end of life in that tormented body, and it was time to move on, to be free of all that pain. Of course she had left—it was the same thing I had felt with Dorothy years before—and it was totally in character for her not to draw out her good-byes.

So this was how it was, I thought, nodding ruefully and driving, as it seemed, right into the white glaciers of the mountain. The universe did not care what my heart wanted. But far from being a depressing thought, it gave me a jolt of pure excitement. Life really was a cliffside hike, a wave to ride, a ghost story to tell eager children around a campfire. For a moment, before the grief swallowed me up again, I was happy to be alive in a place of such wonder.

• • •

Rem Ryals has worked at Village Books in Bellingham, Washington for fourteen years. Born in Spokane, a graduate of Seattle University, he has also lived in Richland, Olympia, Leavenworth, Port Angeles, and Eastsound. When not escaping into the world of books, he enjoys knitting, meditation, and botany.

Bigfoot Calls

MATTHEW SIMMONS

A blind man tells me that Seattle has the Bigfoot. When he tells me this, I am not sure that it is entirely accurate, but feel it is best to play along.

I am living in Iowa City, marking time between graduation from college and . . . something. I am not sure what's next. It is summer, and I am taking a walk from my apartment to a park off the Iowa River, where at half a dozen baseball fields, a dozen Little League baseball teams are playing.

The blind man is standing by the chemistry building on the University of Iowa campus. He is rocking himself back and forth, standing in a doorway. He is waiting. He is rocking. Mostly, he is listening. He hears me walk by—a flight of stairs behind the chemistry building are a shortcut to the river and the path to the park—and calls out.

"May I shake your hand?" he says.

It does not occur to me that, sometimes, when someone asks me to do something, I am under no obligation to do it.

He is very large, but he is wearing a teal T-shirt and a matching pair of teal shorts. He has sandals and tall white socks. A dangerous man would not make this footwear choice, I decide. I walk to him and shake his hand. He does not ask me for my name. I return the favor. He holds on to my hand after the shake. He says he hears a noise. He can't find the source of the noise. He asks if I would help him find the noise.

Let me reiterate: it does not occur to me that, sometimes, when someone asks me to do something, I am under no obligation to do it.

We walk down the stairs to the river—his cane under his arm, his hand on my elbow, him stepping down feet together, apart, together, apart—along the path and try to discover the source of the noise. (I am not yet sure to what noise he is referring. A whirring? A whooshing? He is imprecise in his description of it.)

The stairs are surrounded by trees. The blind man claps his hands together and makes a whoop. "We're in the woods," he says.

I tell him that we are in the woods, and that, also, very soon I will have to go home and call my brother, so I can only help him locate the noise for a short period of time.

"Where does your brother live?" he asks.

I tell him that my brother lives in Seattle.

"Oh," he says. "They have the Bigfoot out there. Has he seen the Bigfoot?"

I'm not sure. I tell him I'm not sure. I tell him that maybe I will ask my brother when I call him.

"They have the Bigfoot out there," he says. "You should see if he's seen him. Whoop. We're still surrounded by trees." The blind man, I think, is echolocating. "We don't have the Bigfoot here."

As we walk, I accidentally convince the blind man that my uncle is Bigfoot. "Who," he asks, "is the biggest, tallest man you've ever known?" I tell him it is my uncle. "Does he have lots of hair on his arms and face?" He does, actually. He keeps his lip, chin, and cheeks shaved, but his hair is thick and black, and he always has an impressive late-afternoon shadow. And his arms are covered in hair.

"Does he sometimes come at you? Make like he's going to pick you up and hug you?" Sure. When I was little and we met at family gatherings, he would do this. "Is your uncle in Seattle? In the Northwest?"

My uncle is in Indiana, but the blind man figures he visits my brother in Seattle a lot. And when my uncle visits, the blind man further speculates that he must spend time out in the woods, hiking and appearing briefly to tourists and outdoorsy locals. Lumbering through the brush. Leaving behind footprints in the mud.

I promise the blind man that I will somehow find him if my uncle visits me in Iowa City. The blind man wants very much to meet the Bigfoot.

Every time I speak to my brother on the telephone, he suggests I move out to Seattle, because there are lots of jobs, and many of those jobs pay better than the kind of work I currently have. Also, those jobs involve writing content for websites. It's the '90s, and websites are—we are led to believe—a fine venue for a creative writer's content. For those (like myself) with some training in journalism. None of these things convince me to pack up and move to Seattle. Too big, I decide. I prefer college towns. Small, Midwestern college towns. They seem friendlier. An example: Iowa City had a terrible wind storm blow through town and knock down trees. Power lines were snapped. Block after block was without power. The blackout lasted for three days. As a community, without any prompting from city government, Iowa City decided that this meant it should have a barbecue. Every house had a grill out front. Every refrigerator was emptied. Everyone offered hot dogs to passersby.

"So, you guys have the Bigfoot out there?" I ask next time I get my brother on the phone.

"The what?" he says.

"The Bigfoot. Sasquatch. Cryptozoology's Northwest superstar?"

"I wouldn't know about that. Real Networks, though. We have Real Networks. The Real Networks. They make media players. There's Microsoft. Ever want to be a technical writer? You could do that here."

I persist. "But you like to go hiking, right? And

you've never seen anything? No sightings of the Bigfoot?"

"No, not that. There have been no sightings of the Bigfoot for me since I moved here. Also rare is unnecessary use of the definite article *the*, too," he says. He puts his wife on the phone. She seems to dodge the question of Bigfoot sightings.

It is a couple of years later when I decide I would like to have a job providing content to websites of one kind or another. I decide I would probably enjoy having a job with health care. I load everything I have into a car and drive to Seattle.

On the way, I see the Madonna of the Prairie. She is a little south of Lawrence, Kansas—a tall concrete statue, facing west, a tribute to the pioneer women who traveled in the same direction I am traveling, in search of the same thing I am in search of. I buy a $5 cowboy hat in Colorado because I see a sign every mile for twenty or so miles telling me that I will soon be able to buy a $5 cowboy hat. I see the Martian-esque landscapes of Utah. I fill up my gas tank at a station shaped like a teapot. I drive past the waterfall from David Lynch's television series *Twin Peaks*, Snoqualmie Falls, twenty-five miles outside of Seattle.

Before I get there—possibly while I am driving through Idaho—the Internet bubble bursts and all the jobs disappear. There are no longer websites looking for content. Not my kind, anyway. I hear that, hidden beneath the bubble's façade, there is a more stable, if not as lucrative, avocation. Seattle is a town full of readers. I find a job at a bookstore.

I find a place to live in a neighborhood that is a lot like a college town. It's much greener than I had expected. Even in summer, when the lawns of my Midwestern homes are burnt brown and tan, the plants in Seattle are green. There are trees everywhere. People take pride in their gardens. I walk from place to place. My neighborhood is on a ridge in the northern part of the city. It is like Seattle's spine, its arched back. The neighborhoods in Seattle are body parts. There are limbs. There is a posterior south of me. Farther south, enormous feet, perhaps.

I cannot say for certain, but it seems to me Seattle is happier without the bubble. Without the tech boom. Seattle seems happier concentrating on its flora instead of its temporary digital explosion. I feel certain that I am better off selling books to people who want to read than I would be creating content. I feel that now, years later, I would be empty of content, anyway. There would be none left in me.

A short bike ride from my home puts me in the woods. Sometimes I close my eyes and clap my hands together, or make a little whoop. I am surrounded by trees. I want to stand in place and rock back and forth. I want to shake the Bigfoot's hand.

• • •

Matthew Simmons is the author of the novella *A Jello Horse* (Publishing Genius Press, 2009). He is The Man Who Couldn't Blog (themanwhocouldntblog.blogspot.com), interviews editor for the journal *Hobart* (hobartpulp.com), and a regular contributor to HTML Giant (htmlgiant.com). He lives in Seattle with his cat, Emmett, and is the copywriter at University Book Store, celebrating its 110th anniversary of independent bookselling in 2010.

Dreaming of Rain

SARAH HUTTON

It was the summer of 1994 when my friends and I got obsessed with the idea of Seattle. We were fifteen, sixteen years old, scholarly girls who lived in the parched, sun-flooded desert of Las Vegas. When *Nevermind* came out a few years earlier, we sat dumbfounded as the radio played our new soon-to-be anthem. We scrounged together our babysitting money and hoarded allowances to buy the CD. We listened and nodded and mumbled along with the lyrics, and our dreams began right there.

That summer though, that's when the dreams started taking hold. We would move to Seattle. Kurt Cobain had just died and *Time* magazine had just featured Seattle on its cover, how it was the hip place to be. I don't remember having *Time* around the house: maybe I saw it on the racks at the grocery store, maybe at the doctor's office. Somehow I got my hands on a copy. I read the article over and over, cut out the picture of the misty, illuminated skyline at night and taped it up on my wall. We were at the age when kids start rustling their untested wings, eager to take flight. Colleges were sending fat information packets to our homes, luring us with their lush campuses and stately buildings. Our favorite place to dream was a small park by my friend B's house. We would go to 7-11, buy enormous cups of coffee loaded with ounces of sugar, and sit on the swings, the tails of our flannels flapping behind us with our motion.

It's hard to convey how strongly this vision had taken over our brains. We made lists of reasons why Seattle was so cool ("The buses are free!" "Jimi Hendrix came from there!"), we studied maps of the city, we looked up apartment prices. When something particularly annoying and Vegas-based occurred, like our thighs sticking to the bus bench from the heat or our eyes scratched raw from the dust storms, one of us would say, "It won't be like this..." and the other two would chime in,

". . . when we live in Seattle!"

Through the fiscal magic of grants and scholarships, loans and parental generosity, I made it to Seattle. The months before my departure I dreamt of nothing but rain and I began to cast a slightly nostalgic eye on my current surroundings. Although I was glad to be leaving Vegas, I was even more glad to be going to a place I had dreamed of for so long. I had been to Washington before on road trips and pre-college visits, but it only took me a few days to know I was home.

My school had one of those bonding sessions in the woods before the start of the quarter, and, although I did bond with a couple of people, it was more of an introduction to the land. Trees, trees, trees—more trees than one could ever imagine fitting into one space. Everything was wet, too: the ground, my clothes, the windows, they all held the permanent moisture. And the light, even when sunny, was a muted form, a filtered shade.

We went on nature walks and had meditation time, and with each new foray I found something different. Leaves the size of my face, curtains of moss the most vibrant green you could dream of, spiderwebs laden with dew that made them visible for yards in every direction. Everything was so dense and lush—especially compared to the harsh, bright-light desert I had called home a week before—that my brain went a little haywire. Part of me wanted to walk right into the forest, lie down on a mossy rock, and watch the animals, insects, and sky until I, too, was covered with green. Another part of me, the atavistic self-preserving part, kept to the well-worn paths for fear of being swallowed whole by the wildness of it all.

I was a little relieved when we returned to the city. This was what I had studied; this was the framework for my dreams. What the maps did not show and that I did not remember from previous visits was how damn hilly the city is. When someone says, "Go up four blocks," they often mean it literally, a palpable change in altitude. I spent many months negotiating those hills until I figured out the flattest routes to my most frequent destinations.

And of course, the coffee. Now, when there's a Starbucks on every block in every city and push-button lattes in every gas station, it's hard to imagine that a city was known for so many cafés, carts, and restaurants serving the wonderful elixir called espresso. There were easily a dozen places to get coffee within a five-minute walk of my dorm.

When confronted with my first chalkboard menu, I felt like an absolute rube surrounded by the language of doppio and Americano. (Later, when I became a barista, I had a little pity for the tourists who had no clue. But only a little.) I also didn't realize how different each café could be. Café Paradiso became a quick favorite because of its proximity and its music. Vivace had an older, more pretentious crowd but also had, hands down, the best-trained baristas on Capitol Hill. Four Angels was very small and bright, and had the best hot chocolate. Bauhaus was its opposite, a glass-walled yet very dark industrial-feeling space where my friends and I would gather for marathon writing sessions fueled by quadruple lattes and Ding-Dongs that glittered in their silver wrappers next to the muffins and biscotti. (One time when I wasn't there, my friend sat next to August Wilson. We had just seen *Seven Guitars* and had our minds blown. I was so jealous I almost cried.)

Later, when I moved out of the dorms and into my

own place, I grew attached to B&O, which on weekend mornings was a great brunch spot and on weekend evenings was the place for all the theater- and opera-goers to stop and get some dessert, but the rest of the time was taken over by students and artists.

I acclimated to Seattle quickly. The umbrella (touristy) and poncho (dorky) were quickly relegated to the back of the closet. I learned to dress in layers, something I did not understand until I started watching my fellow classmates and their intricate peeling of temporarily unneeded garments.

And of course, the rain. I think the rain is the first thing that people think of when they think of the Northwest. What eludes most is the constantness of it. In most places, "rain" is a finite weather pattern. You can say, "Oh, it started raining," and then an hour or two later look out the window and say, "Oh, it stopped." Just as the Eskimos have dozens of words for snow, there are dozens of words for rain here, from misting to spitting to drizzling to pouring. Each carries its own nuances.

And even if it is not raining, the sky is often gray for months at a time. It has its own beauty in a way, the flatness of color, the shifting of clouds, the muted light, but some people just can't handle it. There was one year, early 1999 I think, where the region had had more than one hundred successive days with precipitation of some kind. Three straight months. I was talking to my mom on the phone during this period about how wretched the weather was, even by Seattle standards, and I said, "I'm starting to understand why people jump off the Space Needle." (I realize in hindsight this was not the best thing to say to a worry-prone mother.) A few days later, a box with PRIORITY MAIL stamped all over it was waiting for me. My mom had sent me a Sun Box: Sun-Maid raisins, sun-dried tomatoes, sunglasses, sundae toppings, lip balm with sunscreen, Sunkist oranges, and some chocolates wrapped in smiling sun foil. I lined the items up on my kitchen counter like an altar. The sun finally did break through a few days later. (Coincidence?)

After so long under a wet blanket of gray, when the sun finally does come out the only words to describe it are spiritual in nature: divine, miraculous, a blessed event. In late February there is often a day or two that qualifies as absolutely gorgeous. At first it seems like a trick, but then you realize—it's true! The sun is out! And the newly acquired vitamin D courses through your body and everybody is outside. Bicycles, Frisbees, footballs, everything is dusted off. Smiles broaden and shoulders unhunch. There's a sort of contained mania to those days, and the next morning when you wake up and look out the window at gray and drizzle, you shrug and say, "Well, that was fun," and grab your rain boots again.

I'm not a real outdoorsy person. That definitely puts me in the minority here. Hiking, kayaking, cycling—the trails and waterways are full of people pursuing these healthy endeavors. I'm much more of a quiet indoor reader type. The number of bookstores here was unbelievable to me at first. There was one, Twice Sold Tales, just a few blocks from campus, that was open twenty-four hours on Fridays and Saturdays. My friend Ryan and I would walk over at some ridiculous time and spend hours browsing the stacks. We are both voracious readers and night owls, so this became our second home, complete with cats.

A lot of my peers were creative jaded types who always found something to complain about: the lack of good music, the crappiness of the buses, anything really, even if it wasn't true. I'd mumble a fake agreement, but inside I was overjoyed to be living in a city where buses ran at frequent intervals along the main routes of the city and live music could be found every night of the week. It's hard to be jaded and elated at the same time.

I tried to live outside of Washington as an adult. I lived in Las Vegas again for a few years and was quite miserable. I still had my friends and family there, but after years of living with the green and rain and gray, Vegas was an assault on the senses, the equivalent of a cartoon frying pan to the head. Everything shimmered with the unreal heat and the trees were either hopeful upstarts planted in new subdivisions or palm trees that are ridiculous in the first place. I only lasted two years before I hauled everything back to Washington.

Now I live in Bellingham, in the very northwest corner of the state, about twenty minutes from the Canadian border. It's a perfect fit: all of the coffee, books, and people like Seattle but without the city bustle. There's no real rush hour here; nobody really rushes anywhere, come to think of it. I'm even more outnumbered as a non-outdoorsy person here, but that's okay, too. The sky is still white-gray, and the trees are just as incredible as the first time I saw them. I get down to Seattle a few times a year, and my heart still gives a little flutter when I see the skyline emerging, reminding me of the dream-filled girl who found her home.

• • •

Sarah Hutton graduated from Seattle University with a B.A. in English and philosophy. She is currently the store manager and children's book buyer for Village Books in Bellingham, Washington. She still likes the rain.

The Rock

ANN COMBS

The grass is still green here on Bainbridge Island, perhaps not greener than it used to be, but green nonetheless.

Teenagers who live here refer to it as "The Rock," as in: "I can't wait to get off The Rock." "There's nothing to do here on The Rock." "Why do I have to live on The Rock?" But once they grow up, move away, and have families of their own, they realize they would sell their souls to the devil to move back to The Rock.

By then, however, it's too late. Housing prices have shot up out of reach because Californians and people from the East Coast look on us as a fine location for a second or third home. "We can spend July there," they reason, "perhaps even part of August." So they build

8,000-square-foot homes that stand empty a good part of the year, especially in November, when the fog is thick, the rain is constant, and roofs begin to leak. And island alumni continue to look longingly back at The Rock as they raise their families on the mainland.

Across Puget Sound, folks in Seattle and Bellevue think we're the answer to city living. "Ah, to be in the country," they jubilate. "The peace, the quiet, the trees, the wildlife. And yet we'll be just a half hour's ferry ride from the opera, the ballet, and shopping in the city." So they move here, cut down the six or eight second-growth Douglas firs they claim are blocking their view of the water, and begin the futile search for ways to keep the deer out of their yards. And they become accustomed to missing the last pas de deux of the ballet and the last aria of the opera because they don't want to miss the late ferry.

To those of us who have lived here since twenty minutes after God invented dirt, however, the island is just the island. It isn't the same island it was when my parents and I first moved here toward the end of World War II. When we came and settled down in the house that had once belonged to the foreman at Port Blakely Mill, things were fairly simple. Houses were modest; ours got indoor plumbing a few years after we moved in. A space heater in the dining room was our source of warmth, a great deal of warmth, but only in the dining room, and not much in the rest of the house. Outside, there were gorgeous trilliums on the hill behind the house, and a beach in our front yard. Waves lapped up against the shore, which, along with the sound of the wind in the trees, lulled us to sleep at night.

There weren't a lot of ball fields or open gym hours in those days. But we didn't lack for exercise. We rode bikes up to Eagledale, and because the ferry docked both there and in Winslow, we could hitch a ride across Eagle Harbor and then pedal the four or five miles home. We also rowed all around the bay. We rowed out to Blakely Rocks to gather clam shells to strew on the paths around the property. And every Wednesday, when my mother was coming back from her weekly jaunt into Seattle, my father rowed us out to the channel marker to wave at her as the ferry passed by.

In the summer, we swam, but not in a pool with regulated temperatures and disinfectants. We swam in the bay with the kelp and the seaweed. We built a raft, a new one each year, from which we leaped, dove, and jumped with abandon. The water was always icy cold—it varies two degrees from winter to summer—so there was no strolling in to splash daintily and then duck down. It was, "OK—one, two, three, yikes!" Since the beach was so rocky, we had to wear tennis shoes just to get to the shore's edge. And we amused ourselves with beach fires at night. Anyone with a hot dog stick, a guitar, and the ability to remember all the verses of "Clementine" or "The Eddystone Light" was more than welcome.

On occasion we went to the movies. There were no cineplexes then; no first-run movies debuted on Bainbridge Island. The Lynwood Theater was the only movie house, with films maybe two or three years old, films which often split or burned up halfway through. But that was all right. I gasped as Ronald Reagan croaked, "Where are my legs?" in *Kings Row*. I thrilled during *State Fair* at the singing of "It's a Grand Night for Singing."

I know I am being nostalgic for simpler times, and I

really do appreciate the fact that the island has come of age, with new and varied inns, restaurants and bakeries, bookstores, clothing shops and antique stores. The woods my children played in have been cut down and are now the site of a condo complex, but there are still plenty of parks and trails all over the island.

Still, even with all the progress, with the mansions, the condominiums, and the occasionally surly drivers grumbling about no parking, some things haven't changed. The power goes out every now and then; November, December and January are still rain-soaked; and we still plan our comings and goings around the ferry schedule.

So perhaps we haven't lost our essential character after all. We still have enough of it to call ourselves, affectionately, The Rock.

• • •

Ann Combs lives on Bainbridge Island in the house she and her husband remodeled while raising six children. She's been at Eagle Harbor Books for almost twelve years, peddling books, sifting through other people's used volumes, and monitoring the store's annual limerick contest.

My Washington ID

DAVID K. WHEELER

My Washington driver's license arrived in the mail yesterday. After living here for nearly four years, I figured it was about time I applied for one—now that I've graduated from college, live in a house in Bellingham, and have been employed in a few positions, including bookseller at Village Books. Before, I was just the out-of-state college student from Idaho, a novelty to friends and roommates who have always lived in Washington. Where I grew up, we were less than four miles from Washington as the state goldfinch flies, and when we started attending church in Spokane, I became the token border child.

Forget all that. I'm now officially a resident of this beautiful state, officially; I am no longer just passing as one. I am registered to vote for issues that properly affect me. I will no longer have to wait while Boundary Bay Brewery staff squint at an unfamiliar ID. No, I am just like everyone else and will be served Bellingham's finest microbrews promptly. Although they *could* take a moment to appreciate the quality of the picture; really, it's the best driver's license photo I've ever had. The colors are true and the focus is sharp. And my hair decided it wanted to cooperate that day, despite the temperamental spring snow flurries.

Most of what I've seen of this state has been while I'm driving, from the windows on my '93 Ford Probe. Ever since enrolling at Western Washington University in Bellingham, up in the northwestern corner of the state, I have done my fair share of commuting on holidays and vacations. I remember the summer I went back home after my first year. I had loaded down my car with everything from my dorm room—computer, bedding, clothes, posters, a small piano. There was just room enough for me to sit at the steering wheel; the rest of the car was packed to the hinges, which was fine because I was making the trip alone.

As I passed through the Columbia River Gorge

along Interstate 90, dark clouds hung above me, lumps of rain reaching down among the wind turbines behind me and the Wild Horses Monument to the east. I remember listening to Death Cab for Cutie on the drive. Merely two weekends prior, I had seen this band in concert at the annual Sasquatch Music Festival, the brainchild of Seattlite concert promoter Adam Zacks. At a Memorial Day weekend festival chock-full of incredible acts, Death Cab had been my primary draw. And how perfect it was! They had formed in Bellingham, at the very school I was attending, and now, there they were, performing their music live. For me—more or less. As the sun set into the craggy river gorge behind the stage, I could think of nothing more beautiful than to hear Ben Gibbard's sweet voice crooning *That night, the sun in retreat / Made the skyline look like crooked teeth / In the mouth of the man who was devouring us both.*

As I continued east and listened through the band's third CD, The Photo Album, I nearly cried over the lines from "A Movie Script Ending," the ones that describe downtown Bellingham. The whole album seems like a series of snapshots of the city and served only to remind me what I was leaving for three months. There are those little coffee shops and diners along Railroad Street where I've come to spend much of my free time, the quiet trails that spiderweb all over the city linking neighborhood to city block to lakefront, and the friends I've come to love. There's something in the Bellingham air that tinges every thought with sentiment and sepia, and the magic is there whenever I come back after being gone.

After so many trips home to Idaho, I decided I needed variation, an alternative route; all my previous commutes had been the same up till then. I always took Interstate 5 south from Bellingham to Lynnwood, switched to 405 South, and met up with I-90 just east of Seattle. My logic was that I'd miss all the city traffic, or much of it. But what usually ended up happening was that, along about the boomburb of Bellevue, traffic would come to a crawl, just before the I-90 junction, which put me in a bad mood and left me sour for the next few hours.

So instead, I took Highway 2 at Everett this time, crossing the Cascade Mountains much farther north, at Stevens Pass, a precarious route much of the rest of the year due to the great snowfall causing its already steep grades to ice over. The highway, however, is a more direct route, wending its way across the shifting terrain of Washington, the lush Pacific coast, over the rugged mountains, through plains and apple country, river valleys and deserts. Once through the pass, the road is bespeckled with tiny townships. Most conspicuous seems to be Leavenworth. The Bavarian-style tourist town is enchanting to say the least, right down to their lederhosen.

Nestled between the Cascades and the Wenatchee River and founded by American farmers and gold miners, Leavenworth experienced a rise with the advent of the Great Northern Railway Company, but when the railroad was rerouted, the town fell into bitter decline for nearly thirty years. In the 1960s, they took a risk to save themselves from complete collapse. Their solution: go German! They began transforming the entire town, passing it off as an old Alpine village. Storefronts, resorts, and sidewalks all received a facelift to become the rarest gem of state tourism: a trinket from half a world away. I'll admit I did a double-take when a man decked out in traditional *tracht* crossed the road in front of me, but by the end of my short tour along the main road, the place had grown on me.

Between Leavenworth and Wenatchee are stretches of road populated by apple trees with white skin and gnarled branches, the heart of Washington's apple country. Washington has been leading the country in apple production since the 1920s. Once, while some friends and I were rafting on the Wenatchee River, our guide pointed to some irrigation ducts just visible near the peaks of the surrounding hills. "We call that the apple juice pipeline," he said. "You know Tree Top?" The six of us in the raft nodded. I'm sure he meant it was for irrigating the apple orchards, but I couldn't help but imagine gallons and gallons of apple juice being pumped around the state. Now, every time I pass through the sprawling Wenatchee valley, I think of that—that, and the unassuming chic of agri-tourism.

After Wenatchee, I thought I followed the main highway, the Columbia still to my left sparkling in the summer sun, and eventually ran smack into the Grand Coulee Dam. I recalled coming to the dam before, when I was much younger, and my dad had turned off the main highway to get to the largest concrete structure in the United States. Things of that magnitude, you don't often miss by chance. We had gone there to watch the famous laser light show, which takes its audience through the history of the dam itself, the Columbia River Basin, and the surrounding Native American communities, narrated by none other than the mighty Columbia itself, a booming voice not unlike anything you've heard from James Earl Jones.

I pulled into an information center and made a call. "Dad, I've got a question," I said. "Suppose I'm at Grand Coulee Dam. How far out of the way am I from where I want to be?"

He laughed. This wasn't the first time I'd been lost on a Washington state highway and wouldn't be the last. When I'd gone on a retreat with a group of college friends to Whidbey Island, down along the Puget Sound, I was miles off course in Anacortes when I started questioning my whereabouts. I had arrived at a ferry terminal and was 85 percent sure I did not need to take a ferry to this island; I was almost positive I needed to take a bridge. I was right, but I had been wrong about ten miles back when I had taken Highway 20 Spur instead of staying on Highway 20. In my defense, where I grew up, there was no such thing as a highway "spur."

As I stared at the massive wall in front of me, my dad said, "You probably missed a turn back near Coulee City." A misnomer for the town, really. Coulee City is actually quite a drive from the dam.

"Oh." I frowned. "I suppose I'll be home later than I was planning. Don't hold dinner."

Even though I had no desire to stay and check things out, I was once again stunned by the enormity of Grand Coulee Dam. Built in response to the Great Depression in 1933 to provide jobs as part of the Public Works Administration and Roosevelt's New Deal, the mammoth structure still leads the nation in production of hydroelectricity; in fact, it ranks fifth in the world, and I had stumbled upon it almost by accident.

The highway eventually joined I-90 and descended into Spokane. I joined other eastbound cars, passing a growing number of Idaho license plates. After spending so much time west of the Cascades, where I have come to grips with my ignorance of highways, byways, and spurs, I have more familiarity and ownership here on the east side of the state. For all the hot weekends in June I spent watching my brother play Hoopfest, 3-on-

3 basketball in downtown Spokane; for the holidays we crossed the Cascade Mountains in blinding snowstorms to visit family; and for the errands we ran all over Spokane County nearly every Saturday, I feel as though I have always been as much a Washington resident as I have been of Idaho.

I'll admit that it is indeed strange to relinquish residency in a state I lived in for so long. But to become a resident of Washington seems only natural to me. While Idaho stays somewhere in my murky gut, I am assimilating to the charmed variety Washington has to offer. Maybe I dream of a stint as a performing Seattle musician. Maybe I have a little more city in me than the Idaho panhandle can accommodate. Although nothing of a seafarer, I prefer the ocean inlets and seaside communities along the Washington coast to the landlocked Idaho prairies. So whether at the voting booth or the Boundary Bay Brewery, waiting in line at the grocery store or the bank, I know my ID reflects what I am rapidly and authentically becoming: more than just a passer-by.

• • •

David K. Wheeler is a former bookseller at Village Books in Bellingham, Washington, as well as a writer. His work has been published in literary journals such as *The Penwood Review* and *Jeopardy Magazine*. He is currently working on his first novel and contributes to the Burnside Writers Collective at www.burnsidewriters.com.

The Wilmot Memorial Library

SUSAN SCOTT

When I was quite young, in the mid-1950s, I spent a great deal of time with my grandparents, who lived just three doors down from the Wilmot Memorial Library in Seattle's Wallingford neighborhood. The library was housed in a bungalow left to the city in the owner's will, with the adult collection in the living room, children's books in the dining room, and mysteries and westerns back in what had been the kitchen.

My grandparents were voracious readers. My granddad was a regular visitor to the bungalow, checking out tall stacks of books each time, which he always deliberately kept a day or two past their due date; he thought the library could use the money. In those days, long before computers, you checked out a book by writing your library card number on the narrow card in the book's fly-leaf pocket, handing it to the librarian, then receiving a rubber-stamped date-due card in return.

My granddad had grown impatient with this system, particularly since he checked out so many books at one time, and had eventually badgered the good librarians into keeping his library card under glass at the big front desk. He just collected the due-date cards and handed them over to the obliging ladies of Wilmot. If they thought he was a pain in the neck, they were too nice to say so.

At a very tender age—those were simpler times—I was allowed to visit the library alone since it was so nearby. And when it was time to check my books out, I'd been instructed to explain that my granddad's library card was there, under the glass—I could barely reach high enough to point—and I was allowed to use it. This worked well unless there was a new employee who had not yet been introduced to the eccentric borrower down the block, let alone his very young granddaughter. The whole story had to be explained all over again and a coworker fetched to corroborate, before I'd be allowed to leave with my books. I took to looking straight at the desk when I walked in, to see if I needed to gird my four-year-old self to break in another rookie on this visit.

Eventually, I asked one of the library ladies if I couldn't have my own card. "Well, you could," she said, "but you'd have to be able to write your name." Well, that was no problem, I quickly explained; I'd been able to write my name for ages. She looked at me skeptically, but the four- or five-year old girl before her could, obviously, write her name and indeed read, so the form was duly filled out, and on my next visit to my grandparents, I skipped happily down the street to pick up my newly minted Seattle Public Library card. As it was handed over, the librarian told me I was the youngest person in town to have one!

Naturally, I was very proud at the time, and as the years have gone by, there has always been a library card in my wallet. My first job was at the Northeast Branch, not so very many years later. And now, as a bookseller, I haven't strayed too far from these bibliographic beginnings. But my favorite part of the story is the flexibility of all the parties involved, most especially the Wilmot

Memorial Library staff. Our much faster-paced, more standardized and regulated world today rarely affords an opportunity for this kind of institutional improvisation.

But when it does, I always say the same thing: This is the way the world should work.

• • •

Susan Scott worked in advertising in Seattle and New York before beginning her bookselling career at the legendary Books & Co. in New York City. She and her husband returned to Seattle in the late 1980s, where they raised their daughter and son. Unable to resist this beguiling profession, she continued her career at Queen Anne Avenue Books and, for the past thirteen years, at the Secret Garden Bookshop, where she is a buyer/manager.

ABFFE
275 Seventh Avenue New York, New York 10001
www.abffe.com 212-587-4025

March 2010

Dear Reader,

Thank you! By purchasing this book, you have contributed to the fight for free speech in the United States. HarperCollins is donating a portion of the proceeds to the American Booksellers Foundation for Free Expression (ABFFE), the bookseller's voice in the fight against censorship.

ABFFE fights censorship legislation at the state and federal levels. It is a leader in the fight to protect the privacy of bookstore records and is currently campaigning to restore the safeguards for reader privacy that were eliminated by the USA Patriot Act. In conjunction with the National Coalition Against Censorship, it sponsors the Kids' Right to Read Project, which opposes the hundreds of challenges to books that occur in schools and libraries every year. ABFFE is a sponsor of Banned Books Week, the only national promotion of the freedom to read.

We appreciate your support!

Sincerely yours,

Chris Finan
President

THE PACIFIC NORTHWEST INDEPENDENT BOOKSELLERS ASSOCIATION

LIST OF BOOKSELLERS

ALASKA

Anchorage Museum Shop
121 W 7th Ave, Anchorage, AK, 99501
907-343-6139 www.anchoragemuseum.org

Babbling Book
223 Main St., Haines, AK, 99827
907-766-3356

Fireside Books
720 South Alaska Street, Palmer, AK, 99645
907-745-2665, www.goodbooksbadcoffee.com

Gulliver's Books Inc
3525 College Rd, Fairbanks, AK, 99709
907-474-9575, www.gullivers-books.com

Hearthside Books
8745 Glacier Hwy, Nugget Mall, Juneau, AK, 99801
907-789-2750, www.hearthsidebooks.com

Homer Bookstore,
332 E. Pioneer Ave #1, Homer, AK, 99603
907-235-7496

The Next Page
3833 East Rezanof, Kodiak, AK, 99615
907-481-7243

Old Harbor Books, Inc.
201 Lincoln St, Sitka, AK, 99835
907-747-8808

Parnassus Books
#5 Creek St, Ketchikan, AK, 99901
907-225-7690, www.ketchikanbooks.com

River City Books & Espresso
43977 Sterling Hwy, Soldotna, AK, 99669
907-260-7722

Skagway News Depot & Books
264 Broadway, Skagway, AK, 99840
907-983-3354, www.skagwaybooks.com

U. of Alaska Anchorage Bookstore
2905 Providence Ave, Anchorage, AK, 99508
907-786-4782, www.uaa.alaska.edu

IDAHO

...and Books, too!
1037 21st St, Lewiston, ID, 83501
208-746-7120, www.andbookstooonline.com

Blue Grouse Books / McCall Drug
PO Box 389, McCall, ID, 83638
208-634-2433, www.mccalldrug.com

Boise State Univ. Bookstore
2249 University Dr., Boise, ID, 83706
208-426-1362, www.boisestatebooks.edu

Bonners Books
PO Box E, 7195 Main, Bonners Ferry, ID, 83805
208-267-2622

Book Shoppe
227 W. Main, Grangeville, ID, 83530
208-983-1248

Iconoclast Books
671 Sun Valley Rd., PO Box 806, Ketchum, ID, 83340
208-726-1564, www.iconoclastbooks.com

Kling's Books
704 Main St, Lewiston, ID, 83501
208-743-8501, www.artandframebydj.net

North Idaho College Bookstore
1000 W. Garden Ave, Coeur d'Alene, ID, 83814
208-769-3364, www.bookstore.nic.edu

Rediscovered Bookshop
7079 Overland Rd., Boise, Id, 83709
208-376-4229, www.rdbooks.org

University of Idaho Bookstore
710 Deakin St, PO Box 444301, Moscow, ID, 83844
208-885-6469, www.bookstore.uidaho.edu

Vanderford's Book & Office
201 Cedar St, Sandpoint, ID, 83864
208-263-2417, www.vanderfords.com

OREGON

Allegory Books & Music
PO Box 249, Gleneden Bch, OR, 97388
541-764-2020

Alpha-Bit
10780 Hwy 126/PO Box 465, Mapleton, OR, 97453
541-268-4310

Annie Bloom's Books
7834 SW Capitol Hwy, Portland, OR, 97219
503-246-0053, www.annieblooms.com

Armchair Books
39 SW Dorion, Pendleton, OR, 97801
541-276-7323

Audubon Society of Portland Store
5151 NW Cornell Rd, Portland, OR, 97210
503-292-9453, www.audubonportland.org

Beach Books
37 S. Edgewood St., Seaside, OR, 97138
503-738-3500, www.beachbooks37.com

Betty's Books
1813 Main St, Baker City, OR, 97814
541-523-7551

Between The Covers
645 NW Delaware Ave., Bend, OR, 97701
541-385-4766, www.btcbooks.com

Bloomsbury Books
290 East Main Street, Ashland, OR, 97520
541-488-0029

Bob's Beach Books
1747 NW Hwy 101, Lincoln City, OR, 97367
541-994-4467, www.bobsbeachbooks.com

Book Darts/Artifacts
3945 Willow Flat Rd., Hood River, OR, 97031
541-354-2230, www.bookdarts.com

Book Dock
PO Box 2006, Harbor, OR, 97415-0300
541-469-6070, www.thebookdock.com

Book Ends
5957 NW Alfalfa Dr., Portland, OR, 97229
971-327-8092

Book Stop: The Neighborhood Bookshop
13 Oak Street, Hood River, OR, 97031
541-386-7867, www.gorgebookstop.com

Bookloft
107 E Main St, Enterprise, OR, 97828
541-426-3351, www.bookloftoregon.com

Books 'N' Bears
PO Box 2326/1255 Bay St, Florence, OR, 97439
541-997-5979

Books on Main
319 East Main St, Cottage Grove, OR, 97424
541-942-7423

Broadway Books, Inc.
1714 NE Broadway, Portland, OR, 97232
503-284-1726

Camalli Book Company, LLC
1288 SW Simpson, Ste C, Bend, OR, 97702
541-323-6134, www.camallibookcompany.blogspot.com

Cannon Beach Book Company
PO Box 1098, Cannon Beach, OR, 97110
503-436-1301, www.cannonbeachbooks.com

Canyon Way Bookstore
1216 SW Canyon Way, Newport, OR, 97365
541-265-8319

Castlemere Books For Children
575 First St., Astoria, OR, 97103
503-325-4590, www.castlemerebooks.com

Children's Place
4807 NE Fremont, Portland, OR, 97213
503-284-8294, www.achildrensplacebookstore.com

Circuit Rider Books Inc.
439 SE Pine St. , Dallas, OR, 97338
800-637-3949, www.circuitriderbooks.org

Cosmic Monkey Comics
5335 NE Sandy Blvd, Portland, OR, 97213
503-253-2752, www.cosmicmonkeycomics.com

Far Country Books
PO Box 988, Pacific City, OR, 97135
503-965-6911

Godfather's Books
1108 Commercial, Astoria, OR, 97103
503-325-8143

Good Books NW
3441 SW Dolph Ct., PO Box 80134, Portland, OR, 97280
503-753-0101, www.gooddivorcebooks.com

Graham's Book & Stationery
PO Box 568, Lake Oswego, OR, 97034
503-636-5676

Grass Roots Books & Music
227 SW Second St, Corvallis, OR, 97333
541-754-7668, www.grassrootsbookstore.com

Green Bean Books
1600 NE Alberta Street , Portland, OR, 97211
503-954-2354, www.greenbeanbookspdx.com

Jan's Paperbacks
18095 SW T.V. Hwy, Aloha, OR, 97006
503-649-3444, www.janspaperbacks.com

John V. Henley
Books & Appraisals, 4715 NE 13th., Portland, OR, 97211
503-351-0809

Klindt's Booksellers & Stationers
315 E. 2nd St., The Dalles, OR, 97058
541-296-3355, www.klintsbooks.com

Murder by the Book
3210 SE Hawthorne Blvd, Portland, OR, 97214
503-232-9995, www.mbtb.com

Oregon Books & Games, LLC
937 NE "D" St, Ste C, Grants Pass , OR, 97526
541-476-3132, www.oregonbooks.com

OSU Bookstore, Inc.
2301 SW Jefferson Ave, PO Box 489, Corvallis, OR, 97339
541-737-0045, www.osubookstore.com

OSU Hatfield Marine Science Center
2030 Marine Science Dr., Newport, OR, 97365
541-867-0126, www.hmsc.orst.edu

North by Northwest Books
6334 S. Hwy 101 #9, Lincoln City, OR, 97367
541-994-3087

Pastiche Inc.
34558 Berg Rd. Warren, OR, 97053
503-366-2631

Paulina Springs Books
252 W Hood Ave, Sisters, OR, 97759
541-549-0866

Paulina Springs Books
422 SW 6th St., Redmond, OR, 97756
541-526-1491

Portland Spirit
110 SE Caruthers, Portland, OR, 97214
503-224-3900, www.portlandspirit.com

Portland State Bookstore
1715 SW Fifth Ave, Portland, OR, 97201
503-226-2631x242, www.psubookstore.com

Powell's at PDX
7000 NE Airport Way #2250, Portland, OR, 97218
503-228-4651 x8018, www.powells.com

Powell's Books for Home & Garden
3747 SE Hawthorne Blvd, Portland, OR, 97214
503-235-3802, www.powells.com

Powell's City of Books
7 NW 9th Ave., Portland, OR, 97209
503-228-0540, ext 453, www.powells.com

Powell's Hawthorne
3723 SE Hawthorne Blvd, Portland, OR, 97214
503-238-1668, ext. 7705, www.powells.com

Reed College Bookstore
3203 SE Woodstock Blvd, Portland, OR, 97202
503-788-6659, www.bookstore.reed.edu

River Run Books
18989 NE Marine Dr #C-30, Portland, OR, 97230
503-667-6830, www.dicksriverrunbooks.com

Some Bookstore in Sandy
39080 Pioneer Blvd, Sandy, OR, 97055
503-668-9640

St. Helens Book Shop
2149 Columbia Blvd., St Helens, OR, 97051
503-397-4917, www.sthelensbookshop.com

Sunriver Books & Music
PO Box 1990, Building 25 #C, Sunriver, OR, 97707
541-593-2525, www.sunriverbooks.com

Tamastslikt Cultural Institute
72789 Hwy 331, Pendleton, OR, 97801
541-966-1982, www.tamastslikt.org

Tea Party Bookshop
420 Ferry St. SE, Salem, OR, 97301
503-508-5886, www.teapartybookshop.com

Third Street Books
334 NE Third Street, McMinnville, OR, 97128
503-472-7786, www.thirdstreetbooks.com

Tree House Books
15 N. Main Street, Ashland, OR, 97520
541-482-9616

UO Bookstore / Duck Store
895 E 13th, PO Box 3176, Eugene, OR, 97403
346-4331, www.uobookstore.com

Waucoma Bookstore
212 Oak St, Hood River, OR, 97031
541-386-5353, www.waucomabookstore.com

Willamette Store
900 State St, Salem, OR, 97302
503-370-6315, www.thewillamettestore.com

Wrigley-Cross Books
2870 NE Hogan Rd., Ste. E, Gresham, OR, 97030
503-667-0807, www.wrigleycrossbooks.com

Wy'East Book Shoppe & Art
67195 E Hwy 26, Ste A, Welches, OR, 97067
503-622-1623, www.wyeast-online.com

WASHINGTON

2nd Look Books
2829 E 29th Ave, Spokane, WA, 99223
509-535-6464, www.2ndlookbooks.com

3rd Street Book Exchange
1615 3rd St., Marysville, WA, 98270
360-659-8734, www.thirdstbooks.com

A Book For All Seasons
703 Hwy 2, Leavenworth, WA, 98826
509-548-1451, www.abookforallseasons.com

A Good Book
1014 Main Street, Sumner, WA, 98390
253-891-9692

Auntie's Bookstore
402 West Main, Spokane, WA, 99201
509-838-0206, www.auntiesbooks.com

Bailey-Coy Books
414 Broadway E, Seattle, WA, 98102
206-323-8842

Baker Street Books
PO Box 967, Black Diamond, WA, 98010
360-886-2131, www.bakerstreetbooks.net

Bethel Avenue Book Company
1037 Bethel Ave , Port Orchard, WA, 98366
360-876-7500, www.bethelavebook.com

Book 'N' Brush
518 N. Market Blvd., Chehalis, WA, 98532
360-748-6221

Book & Game Company
38 E Main St #1, Walla Walla, WA, 99362
509-529-9963, www.bookandgame.com

BookBay, PO Box 520
Freeland, WA, 98249-0520
360-331-5404, www.bookbay.com

Bookery
1 Basin Street NW, Ephrata, WA, 98823
509-754-5321

Books on the West
824 Lynnwood Ave NE, Renton, WA, 98056
425-271-6481, www.booksonthewest.com

BookWorks
1510 Third Street, Marysville, WA, 98270
360-659-4997, www.marysvillebookworks.com

Children's Bookshop
225 W Meeker St., Kent, WA, 98033
253-852-0383, www.childrensbookshoponline.com

Cinema Books
4753 Roosevelt Way NE, Seattle, WA, 98105
206-547-7667, www.cinemabooks.net

Corner Shelf
6 N. Main/ PO Box 846, Omak, WA, 98841
509-826-0527

Cover to Cover Books
1817 Main Street, Vancouver, WA, 98660
360-514-0358, www.covertocoverbooks.net

Darvill's Bookstore
PO Box 166, Eastsound, WA, 98245
360-376-2135, www.darvillsbookstore.com

Discover Your Northwest
164 S. Jackson St., Seattle, WA, 98104
206-220-4140, www.nwpubliclands.com

Eagle Harbor Book Co.
157 Winslow Way East, Bainbridge Island, WA, 98110
206-842-5776, www.eagleharborbooks.com

East West Bookshop
6500 Roosevelt Way NE, Seattle, WA, 98115
206-523-3726, www.eastwestbookshop.com

Eastshore Book Shop
12700 SE 32nd St, Bellevue, WA, 98005
425-747-3780

Edmonds Bookshop
111 Fifth Ave South, Edmonds, WA, 98020
425-775-2789, www.edmondsbookshop.com

Elliott Bay Book Company
101 S Main Street, Seattle, WA, 98104
206-624-6600, www.elliottbaybook.com

Fireside Bookstore
116 Legion Way SE, Olympia, WA, 98501
360-352-4006

Fort Nisqually Living History Museum
5400 N. Pearl St. #11, Tacoma, WA, 98407
253-591-5339, www.fortnisqually.org

Fort Vancouver Bookstore
750 Anderson St., Vancouver, WA, 98661
360-992-1824, www.vnhrt.org

Fremont Place Bk Company
621 N 35th Street, Seattle, WA, 98103
206-547-5970, www.fremontplacebooks.com

Friends of Skamokawa Foundation
1394 W State, Skamokawa, WA, 98647
360-795-3007

Garfield Book Co. at PLU
208 Garfield St., Ste 101, Tacoma, WA, 98444
253-535-7665

Griffin Bay Bookstore
PO Box 1669, Friday Harbor, WA, 98250
360-378-5511, www.griffinbaybook.com

Imprint Bookstore Ltd
820 Water St, Port Townsend, WA, 98368
360-385-3643

Inklings Bookshop
5629 Summitview Ave., Yakima, WA, 98908
509-965-5830, www.inklingsbookshop.com

Island Books Etc.
3014 78th SE, Mercer Island, WA, 98040
206-232-6920, www.mercerislandbooks.com

Islehaven Books & Borzoi
210 Lopez Road, Lopez Island, WA, 98261
360-468-2132, www.islehaven.bookscom

Jackson Street Books
823 Bluff Ave., Hoquiam, WA, 98550
360-532-8278, www.jacksonst-books.com

Jerrol's Book & Supply
111 E. University Way, Ellensburg, WA, 98926
509-925-9851, www.jerrols.com

King's Books, Inc.
218 St. Helen's Ave., Tacoma, WA, 98402
253-272-8801, www.kingsbookstore.com

Lesley's Books
240 SW 2nd, Stevenson, WA, 98648
503-278-0959

Liberty Bay Books
18881 D Front St, PO Box 1396, Poulsbo, WA, 98370
360-779-5909, www.libertybaybooks.com

Lindon Bookstore
1528 Cole St, Enumclaw, WA, 98022
360-825-1388, www.lindonbookstore.com

Magnolia's Bookstore,3
06 W. McGraw St., Seattle, WA, 98199
206-283-1062

Math 'n Stuff
8926 Roosevelt Way NE, Seattle, WA, 98115
206-522-8891, www.mathnificent.com

Mockingbird Books
7220 Woodlawn Ave. NE, Seattle, WA, 98115
206-517-9909, www.mockingbirdbooksgl.com

Moonraker Books
209 First St/PO Box 105, Langley, WA, 98260
360-221-6962

Mostly Books
3126 Harborview Ave, Gig Harbor, WA, 98335
253-851-3219, www.mostlybooks.com

Next Chapter
721 S First St/PO Box 574, LaConner, WA, 98257
360-466-2665, www.nextchapter.com

Ninth Moon
8124 150th Pl SE, Snohomish, WA, 98296
360-668-0794, www.gloverinfo@verizon.net

Open Books: A Poem Emporium,
2414 North 45th St, Seattle, WA, 98103
206-633-0811, www.openpoetrybooks.com

Orca Books
509 E 4th Ave Olympia, WA, 98501-1110
360-352-0123, www.orcabooks.com

Out On a Whim Childrens Bookstore,
108 S. 3rd Ave., Yakima, WA, 98902
866-501-7430, www.outonawhimbooks.com

Pacific Mist Books
121 W Washington St, Sequim, WA, 98382
360-683-1396

Paperbacks Galore
1044 14th Ave, Longview, WA, 98632
360-423-9006

Parkplace Books
348 Parkplace Center, Kirkland, WA, 98033
425-828-6546

Pearl Street Books & Gifts
421 N. Pearl St., Ellensburg, WA, 98926
509-925-5678

Pearson Air Museum Bookstore
1115 E. 5th St., Vancouver, WA, 98661
360-694-7026, www.historicreserve.org

Port Book and News
104 East 1st St, Port Angeles, WA, 98362
360-452-6367, www.portbookandnews.com

Queen Anne Avenue Books
1811 Queen Anne Ave. N., Seattle, WA, 98109
206-283-5624, www.queenannebooks.com

Rainbow Books
82 Kessler Lane, Hoquiam, WA, 98550
509-670-3469

Ravenna Third Place Books
6504 20th Ave NE, Seattle, WA 98115
206-525-2347 www.thirdplacebooks.com

Read It Again
11 Palouse St., Wenatchee, WA, 98801
509-662-2093, www.readitagain.biz

Read Me A Story
1419 Commercial Ave., Anacortes, WA, 98221
360-293-4801

Revolution Books
85 S. Washington St. #215, Seattle, WA, 98104
206-325-7415, www.revolutionbookssea.org

Riverwalk Books
116 E. Woodin Ave., PO Box 686, Chelan, WA, 98816
509-682-8901, www.riverwalkbooks.com

Sage Bookstore
116 West Railroad Ave #102, Shelton, WA, 98584
360-426-6011, www.sagebookstore.com

Santoro's Books
7405 Greenwood Ave. North, Seattle, WA, 98103
206-784-2113, www.santorosbooks.com

Seattle Mystery Bookshop
117 Cherry St, Seattle, WA, 98104
206-587-5737, www.seattlemystery.com

Seattle Univ Bookstore
823 12th Ave. , Seattle, WA, 98122
206-296-5823, www.seattleubookstore.com

Secret Garden Bookshop
2214 NW Market St, Seattle, WA, 98107
206-789-5006, www.secretgardenbooks.com

Snow Goose Bookstore
PO Box 939, Stanwood, WA, 98292
360-629-3631

Square One Books
4724 42nd Ave. SW, Seattle, WA, 98116
206-935-5764, www.square1books.com

Suntree Books
1312 N. Woodruff Rd., Spokane , WA, 99206
509-926-3390

Third Place Books
17171 Bothell Way NE, Lake Forest Park, WA, 98155
206-366-3333, www.thirdplacebooks.com

Time Enough Books
157 Howerton Ave, PO Box 682, Ilwaco, WA, 98624
360-642-7667

Tinman Artworks
811 W. Garland, Spokane, WA, 99203
509-325-1500

Top Ten Toys
104 North 85th St, Seattle, WA, 98103
206-782-0098

Trail's End Bookstore
231 Riverside Ave, PO Box 15, Winthrop, WA, 98862
509-996-2345, www.trailsendbookstore.com

Traveler
265 Winslow Way E, Bainbridge Is, WA, 98110
206-842-4578, www.thetraveler.com

University Book Store
4326 University Way NE, Seattle, WA, 98105
206-634-3400, www.ubookstore.com

University Book Store
990 102nd Ave NE, Bellevue, WA, 98004
425-462-4500, www.ubookstore.com

University Book Store
1754 Pacific Ave, Tacoma, WA, 98402
253-272-8080, www.ubookstore.com

University Book Store
15311 Main St., Mill Creek, WA, 98012
425-385-3530, www.ubookstore.com

Vashon Bookshop
17612 Vashon Highway SW, PO Box 2906
Vashon Island, WA, 98070
206-463-2616, www.vashonbookshop.com

Village Books
1200 11th St, Bellingham, WA, 98225
360-671-2626, www.villagebooks.com

Vintage Books
6613 E Mill Plain, Vancouver, WA, 98661
360-694-9519, www.vintage-books.com

Watermark Book Co.
612 Commercial Ave, Anacortes, WA, 98221
360-293-4277

Western Assoc. Students' Bookstore
501 High St Bellingham, WA, 98225
360-650-3958, www.bookstore.wwu.edu

Whodunit? Books
119 E. 5th Ave., Olympia, WA, 98501
360-352-8252

Wide World Books & Maps
4411A Wallingford Ave N, Seattle, WA, 98103
206-634-3453
www.wideworldtravels.com, www.seattlestravelstore.com

Joseph Caldwell's bestselling novel, ***The Pig Did It***, is now in paperback! And the hilarious sequel, ***The Pig Comes to Dinner***, will be available in paperback in April 2010.

"Caldwell's Irish pig is my new love. Caldwell has achieved the impossible with poetic ascents to the peaks of hilarious prose. You will laugh your arse off." —**Malachy McCourt**

In *The Pig Did It*, a pig follows a young American from town to his Aunt Kitty's seaside cottage, where the pig proceeds to uproot the bones of Kitty's lover. A comedy of Irish proportions with a pub scene for the ages and a monumental Irish wake.

In *The Pig Comes to Dinner*, the pig allows Kitty and clan to "see" two tragic visitors from the past in a haunted Irish castle.

"The macabre comedy plays out in sparkling dialogue, with some hilarious speeches that are both incantations of Irish mythology and masterful bits of parody."
—***Washington Post Book World*** (full page review)

PAPERBACK • $13.99
ALSO AVAILABLE IN HARDCOVER

Joseph Caldwell is a playwright and the author of the five well-reviewed novels over almost twenty years. He has been awarded the Rome Prize for Literature by the American Academy of Arts and Letters. He was also a writer on the famous *Dark Shadows* TV show. He has finished Book Three of his Pig Trilogy, coming soon.

MALE OF THE SPECIES, stories by Alex Mindt

"In this remarkable debut, Alex Mindt skillfully portrays a series of unique and compelling worlds. The result is a captivating collection that is a joy to read." **—John Searles**

Clowns, deadbeats, refugees, social climbers all bound by the mysterious ties of fatherhood. Alex Mindt's debut collection is like a chorus of fathers and those they love singing in many accents of the paternal connection that befuddles, enobles, enrages and endures. Each unique voice rings true and clear according to its character.

MERCY, by Alissa York

A gifted Canadian writer makes her debut in the United States with a dark and spellbinding tale of forbidden love.

"York's unflinching but tender eye for the natural world results in graceful ballets of description: butchering techniques have seldom been described in such precise, loving detail, and the flora and fauna of the bog are invested with vibrant individuality."
—Publishers Weekly

VIRGINIA LOVERS, by Michael Parker

In the autumn of 1975, a small town struggles with the mysterious murder of Brandon Pierce, a gay teenager found dead in his parents' bed following a high-school keg party. As Thomas Edgecombe, the editor of the town's newspaper, diligently reports on the crime, he begins to suspect that his two sons may know more about the murder than they're letting on.

THE GREAT LAKES READER

ESSAYS ON THE STATES THAT MAKE THE GREAT LAKES GREAT

"To the multitudes of gratitudes I hold for Midwestern booksellers, I add another—and this time for *their* stories. These are essays that weave the Midwest we know with the Midwest we never suspected."

—MICHAEL PERRY, AUTHOR OF *COOP, TRUCK*, AND *POPULATION: 485*

PAPERBACK • $10.95